AF479843

SELF-PRESERVATION

Self-Preservation today more than ever in a changing world

GABRIEL GIBBENS

TABLE OF CONTENTS

ABOUTH THE AUTHOR

Pen Name: Gabriel Gibbens

For the past 50 years, I have achieved success in various business ventures and dedicated myself to teaching others how to replicate that success. Through my guidance and mentorship, numerous individuals have achieved their goals and created thriving businesses of their own.

One of my greatest passions is engaging in meaningful conversations and writing. I have always found that people love to talk about themselves, and I have honed my skills in asking thought-provoking questions that bring out the best in others. I encouraged my siblings to write down their top 10 life aspirations. I then introduced them to the power of manifestation by having them repeat their wishes daily for a month and, later, once a week. Remarkably, almost all of them achieved 8 out of their ten desired wishes. This experience solidified my belief in the incredible potential of the human mind.

I have even taught poetry and songwriting, and I have had the pleasure of witnessing my students flourish and find their unique voices.

Over the years, I have immersed myself in the writing world, studying various writing styles and techniques. This continuous pursuit of knowledge has allowed me to refine my writing skills and develop a deep appreciation for anyone who puts pen to paper. Additionally, I have been actively involved in a writer's class for the past five years, where I have had the privilege of learning from and collaborating with talented individuals. Many of my classmates have gone on to publish their books or have multiple works under their belts.

While I have found success in business and writing, I also have many hobbies and interests. I have created and sold products on Amazon, Facebook, and Google Ads platforms. Additionally, I have a knack for fixing small appliances and often give them away to those in need. In the past, I also dabbled in jewellery making and participated in various shows, but I have since passed on those creations to others. However, my absolute favourite activity is dancing with my wife. We have been dancing together for 40 years, starting with polka and square dancing in Nebraska and later expanding our repertoire to include ballroom dancing when we moved to Florida.

If you would like to contact me, the best way to reach me is by email at jg40750@gmail.com. I look forward to connecting with you and sharing our passions and interests.

INTRODUCTION

One instinct stands out as being of the utmost importance in the vast fabric of life: self-preservation. The urge to defend oneself and secure survival has been engrained in human nature, from the simplest organisms to the sophisticated humans we are today. Self-preservation is not a single idea; it includes many elements that profoundly influence our daily lives.

In this ground-breaking investigation, we examine the roots of self-preservation and its numerous manifestations in various spheres of life. We explore the complex web of circumstances that have led to the development of this fundamental instinct by drawing on the most recent scientific studies and evolutionary theories.

We unravel the complicated fabric of self-preservation, starting with the primitive instinct to flee from danger and find safety and ending with the complex processes that control our fight-or-flight reactions. But it goes further than that. We also explore this instinct's psychological and social aspects, looking at how it affects our interactions with others, goals, and even our sense of self.

In this enthralling investigation, we set out to comprehend the drive for self-preservation and its broad ramifications. We investigate the evolutionary roots of this impulse, tracking its genesis and locating its occurrences in various facets of life. We learn the tactics and tenets that enable us to protect our well-being and prosper in a constantly evolving society, from physical self-defence to mental and emotional health, from upholding healthy relationships to navigating the digital age.

We learn how to protect ourselves and give ourselves the means to deal with life's challenges with renewed clarity and purpose through a combination of scientific analysis, personal anecdotes, and professional insights. Each chapter examines a different self-preservation aspect and offers helpful suggestions, thought-provoking insights, and doable actions to improve our general well-being.

Join me on this enlightening adventure as we investigate the evolutionary underpinnings of self-preservation, examine its many forms, and learn how it has influenced our past, present, and future. Together, we will discover the strength of self-preservation and set out on a path to a fulfilling and durable life.

This topic explores the evolutionary basis of self-preservation and how it manifests in different facets of life. One aspect of self-preservation is ensuring access to essential resources, such as food. Stocking food is an important consideration for people looking to be self-sufficient during times of crisis. Understanding the instinct of self-preservation is crucial when preparing for potential threats or emergencies.

Non-perishable food items, such as canned goods, dried fruits, and grains, are excellent choices for long-term storage. It is also important to rotate the stock frequently to ensure freshness and prevent waste. Learning about food preservation techniques, such as canning or dehydrating, can further enhance self-preservation efforts.

Another self-preservation aspect is having a secret hideout or haven to escape peril, whether a remote cabin, a fortified underground bunker, or even a hidden room inside your home. The location should be well-stocked with necessities like food, water, medical kits, and communication devices. It is crucial to keep the hideout's location a secret and only share it with trusted people to maintain its effectiveness.

However, it is important to approach this subject with caution and adhere to local laws and regulations. Understanding firearm safety, proper handling, and responsible ownership is paramount. Training in self-defence techniques and obtaining the required permits and licenses can further enhance one's ability to protect oneself and loved ones. Guns and ammunition are frequently considered tools for self-defence and protection.

This topic is of utmost importance today, where personal safety is a growing concern for many people. By learning and practising physical self-defence techniques, individuals can empower themselves and enhance their ability to respond effectively in potentially dangerous situations. Physical self-defence techniques encompass various strategies and techniques to protect oneself physically in various situations.

Martial arts, which include a variety of disciplines with their distinct techniques and philosophies, are one of the most well-liked and efficient forms of physical self-defence. From traditional martial arts like karate and taekwondo to more modern forms like Brazilian Jiu-Jitsu and Krav Maga, martial arts give people the skills and knowledge to defend themselves against potential threats.

Self-defence classes, which are specifically designed to teach practical techniques for personal safety and self-defence and frequently cover a wide range of topics, such as situational awareness, verbal de-escalation, and physical techniques for escaping or neutralizing an attacker, are another invaluable resource for people looking to improve their physical self-defence skills in addition to martial arts.

Being aware of one's surroundings, avoiding isolated or poorly lit areas, and trusting one's instincts are just a few practical tips for personal safety that people can incorporate into their daily lives to reduce the risk of becoming victims of violence or crime. Individuals can also learn how to use common objects as improvised weapons.

Physical self-defence techniques emphasize the importance of prevention and avoidance, not just learning how to fight or overpower an attacker. Individuals can often avoid potentially dangerous situations by being proactive and taking steps to minimize risks.

Visualization, breathing exercises, and mental rehearsal can help people stay focused and make quick decisions when faced with danger. Furthermore, physical self-defence techniques go beyond the physical aspect and encompass mental and emotional preparedness. Developing a strong mindset and remaining calm under pressure is crucial in effectively responding to threatening situations.

Self-Protection On A Mental And Emotional Level

This topic delves into various strategies and practices to help people maintain their mental and emotional well-being. In today's fast-paced and demanding world, it is essential to prioritize our mental and emotional health to navigate through life's challenges successfully.

Stress management techniques, such as deep breathing exercises, meditation, and mindfulness, can help reduce stress levels and promote a sense of calm and relaxation. Stress is a common experience in our daily lives, and if it is not managed, it can harm our mental and emotional health.

Through regular meditation, people can increase their self-awareness, strengthen their capacity to manage stress and cultivate inner peace. Meditation involves focusing the mind and eradicating the thoughts that can contribute to stress.

Instead of reacting impulsively or feeling overwhelmed, people can learn to respond to stressors more measured and compassionately by engaging in mindfulness practices, which involve being fully present in the moment and non-judgmentally observing one's thoughts, feelings, and sensations.

Self-care is not selfish but a necessary practice to maintain overall well-being and is a crucial component of mental and emotional self-preservation. Examples of self-care practices include engaging in hobbies, spending time in nature, practising gratitude, and engaging in activities that bring joy and fulfilment. Talking to oneself can also be a helpful self-care practice.

Celebrating and acknowledging our accomplishments, no matter how small, can boost self-confidence and give a sense of accomplishment. By focusing on our wins, we can cultivate a positive outlook and maintain motivation and resilience in the face of challenges.

Establishing consistent routines and habits can give our lives a sense of stability and structure. It can include maintaining a regular sleep schedule, exercising frequently, and using healthy stress-reduction techniques. Consistency helps create a sense of control and stability, enhancing general mental and emotional well-being.

THE EVOLUTION OF SELF-PRESERVATION

From simple single-celled organisms to complex human societies, self-preservation has evolved in fascinating ways. This essay explores the evolution of self-preservation, tracing its origins from fundamental biological instincts to the complex moral and ethical considerations that arise in contemporary human society.

The Biological Basis

Infant Life Forms

Chemotaxis, the movement towards or away from specific chemicals, enables these organisms to seek out beneficial environments and avoid harmful ones, illustrating the basic principles of self-preservation. Self-preservation is deeply rooted in biology and is evident in the simplest organisms, such as bacteria.

Function of Instinct

Instinctual behaviors hardwired into an organism's genetic code, became essential for survival. Predatory animals developed hunting instincts, while prey evolved mechanisms for escape and camouflage. These instincts served as foundational elements for the ongoing evolution of self-preservation. As life forms grew more complex, so did their strategies for survival.

The Development of Sensibility

Higher-order animals, like mammals, started to experience the instinct to survive and the emotions associated with it—fear, anxiety, and a sense of self—which acted as a driving force to ensure the continuation of the species. With the evolution of more advanced organisms, self-preservation became entwined with the emergence of sentience.

Cultural and Social Influences

Social Creatures

Social animals like wolves and primates are examples of the collective approach to self-preservation, relying on group dynamics and cooperation. The emergence of cooperative behaviours, such as group hunting or communal defence, to enhance individuals' survival odds marked the development of social structures in some species.

The Human Race

The concept of self-preservation extended beyond individual survival to include preserving family, tribe, and, eventually, entire civilizations. Homo sapiens formed communities and developed complex cooperation, governance, and ethics systems.

Moral and Philosophical Issues To Think About

Moral Conundrums

Immanuel Kant argued for the intrinsic value of human life and the duty to preserve it. At the same time, utilitarian philosophers like John Stuart Mill considered the greater good and the sacrifices that might be necessary. Questions regarding the extent to which one should prioritize one's survival over the well-being of others became central to ethical philosophy.

The Trolley Conundrum

In the famous thought experiment, the Trolley Problem, one must choose whether to divert a runaway trolley to save five people while knowingly sacrificing one person. The scenario forces people to wrestle with the ethical implications of self-preservation, demonstrating the complex interplay between instinct and moral reasoning.

Ecological Ethics

Environmental ethics examines the moral duties of humans to protect the Earth's ecosystems and species, emphasizing the interconnectedness of all life forms. In this context, self-preservation extends to preserving the planet and its resources. As humans have gained unprecedented control over their environment, questions about the preservation of the planet itself have emerged.

Technological Progress

Improvements in Medicine

The quest for self-preservation now includes utilizing scientific and technological advancements to enhance health and longevity. Modern medicine and technology have revolutionized self-preservation by greatly extending human lifespans and reducing mortality rates from diseases and injuries.

Technology-Enhanced Intelligence And Transhumanism

With the potential for mind uploading, bioengineering, and human-machine integration, individuals have decisions about preserving and enhancing their consciousness and physical abilities. These advancements challenge traditional notions of self-preservation and identity. Artificial intelligence and transhumanism have opened up new frontiers in self-preservation.

Psychological Stances

Fear and Worry

Understanding the intricate psychology behind fear and anxiety sheds light on why people make certain decisions to protect themselves and avoid potential dangers. Fear and anxiety are two of the most primal and powerful emotions that humans experience. These emotions have deep evolutionary roots and have evolved as adaptive responses to threats, ensuring the survival of our species.

Fear acts as a built-in alarm system when a person perceives a threat, such as a predator, a natural disaster, or even a car speeding towards them. The body's "fight or flight" response is activated, resulting in a surge in adrenaline, increased heart rate, heightened senses, and a rush of energy. This physiological response prepares an individual to deal with the perceived threat.

While fear is a reaction to a clear and present danger, anxiety involves anticipating potential future harm. This prolonged state of unease and apprehension can be both adaptive and maladaptive. On the one hand, anxiety can encourage people to take precautions and plan for potential threats, increasing their sense of security.

Individual differences, such as genetics, past experiences, and cognitive factors, further influence the psychology of fear and anxiety. Some people may have a genetic predisposition to anxiety, while others may develop it due to traumatic experiences. Additionally, cognitive biases, such as the tendency to overestimate the likelihood of negative outcomes, can amplify feelings of fear and anxiety.

Individuals may engage in risk-averse behaviors when faced with situations that trigger intense fear, such as avoiding risky activities, seeking safety in numbers, or adhering to well-established routines to minimize potential threats. On the other hand, some individuals may be more prone to taking risks as they experience greater levels of fear and anxiety.

Societies and communities also respond collectively to perceived threats, demonstrating the relationship between self-preservation and fear and anxiety. For example, during a public health crisis, fear and anxiety can motivate people to take preventive measures like wearing masks, social isolation, and getting vaccinated to preserve individual and collective well-being.

Understanding the psychology of fear and anxiety provides valuable insights into why people choose their actions when securing their well-being and adjusting to the challenges of an uncertain world. Fear and anxiety are integral parts of the human experience, deeply connected to the concept of self-preservation, and have evolved as adaptive responses to threats.

Risk Awareness

The way people assess threats and make decisions related to self-preservation is not always rational; as a result, there is a wide range in how people perceive risk. This variability in risk perception has significant implications for public health, safety regulations, and policy-making.

Problems and Ethical Conundrums

Population Increase

Balancing the need for resources, food, and space with environmental sustainability is a complex ethical dilemma that requires addressing issues like overpopulation, resource depletion, and equitable distribution. The global human population continues to rise, posing challenges to self-preservation at both the individual and societal levels.

Technical Perils

Artificial intelligence, biotechnology, and nuclear power are powerful forces that can potentially reshape our world for better or worse. While technological advancement brings enormous benefits and opportunities, it also introduces new and complex risks that can jeopardize our existence.

The Rise of Machine Intelligence in Artificial Intelligence (AI)

Healthcare, transportation, finance, and entertainment are just a few industries where artificial intelligence, or AI, which aims to build machines capable of intelligent reasoning and decision-making, holds incredible promise. However, the unchecked development and deployment of AI can pose significant risks.

As AI systems become more autonomous, there is an increasing risk that they will make decisions at odds with human values and objectives. This could manifest in various ways, from biased algorithmic decisions perpetuating discrimination to AI-driven weapons systems making life-or-death decisions without human intervention.

Responsible AI development and regulation, ensuring that AI systems adhere to ethical standards and human values, transparent oversight, and collaboration between governments, organizations, and experts can all help us maximize the benefits of AI while minimizing the risks that come with it.

A Two-Edged Sword Is Biotechnology.

Although biotechnology has transformed several industries, including agriculture, health, and many others, providing answers to some of humanity's most pressing problems, the ability to alter the genetic makeup of living things raises serious ethical and security concerns.

The use of biotechnology for evil purposes, such as the development of bioweapons, is another alarming risk. Gene editing technologies like CRISPR-Cas9 can modify the human genome, potentially eliminating genetic diseases or enhancing desirable traits. However, they also open the door to unintended consequences, such as unforeseen genetic mutations or the creation of designer babies.

International cooperation, strict regulations, and open research practices are essential to guarantee that biotechnology serves humanity's best interests without jeopardizing our long-term self-preservation.

Utilizing Nuclear Energy While Reducing Risk

Nuclear accidents and the potential for the proliferation of nuclear weapons remain serious threats to international security. On the one hand, nuclear power offers a powerful and efficient source of clean energy, reducing our reliance on fossil fuels and mitigating climate change.

The tragedies at Chornobyl and Fukushima are stark reminders of the catastrophic effects of nuclear accidents, which cause immediate harm and have long-lasting effects on the environment and human health. Furthermore, the proliferation of nuclear weapons technology poses a serious existential risk because nuclear conflict could cause extensive destruction.

Investing in research on advanced reactor designs and nuclear waste management is crucial to mitigate risks while gaining the benefits of this energy source, which calls for strict safety measures, strong regulatory frameworks, and international cooperation.

By prioritizing ethical considerations, international cooperation, and transparency, we can harness the transformative potential of these technologies while minimizing the existential risks they pose.

In a Crisis, Moral Decisions

Here, we delve into some of these historical and contemporary instances, highlighting the profound impact of moral choices in times of crisis. Throughout human history, moments of crisis have demanded that individuals and societies confront difficult moral dilemmas where the pursuit of self-preservation collides with broader ethical considerations. These critical junctures often define our collective character and set the course for the future.

The Titanic's Destruction

As the ship sank, the few available lifeboats raised agonizing questions about who should be saved; however, the principle of "women and children first" prevailed, reflecting a societal commitment to protect the most vulnerable. However, the moral compass that guided these decisions reflected a broader commitment to valuing human life above all else, even in dire circumstances.

Jewish Holocaust

Adolf Hitler's regime systematically targeted and executed innocent people based on ethnicity, religious beliefs, or political affiliations. Many people faced the moral choice of collaborating, resisting, or remaining silent in the face of these atrocities. The Holocaust is one of the darkest chapters in human history, where the pursuit of self-preservation was perverted into the mass extermination of millions.

Challenges of the Present: Climate Change

The moral choices related to climate change revolve around intergenerational equity, resource allocation, and responsibility. As we deal with the effects of environmental degradation, individuals and nations must choose whether to prioritize short-term economic interests or take action to preserve the planet for future generations. Climate change highlights the inequity between the sexes and the inability to act responsibly.

Pandemics are one of the modern challenges.

Governments and healthcare systems worldwide had to make decisions about allocating limited medical resources, imposing restrictions on individual liberties, and prioritizing public health over individual liberties. These decisions were fraught with ethical considerations, such as balancing the need to save lives with preserving economic stability and civil liberties. The COVID-19 pandemic has exemplified how societies confront moral dilemmas during crises.

Leading with Morality

Moral leadership's importance is evident in historical and contemporary crises, as leaders' decisions can have far-reaching effects. Leaders who embody ethical principles and prioritize the greater good can inspire positive collective action. In contrast, leaders prioritizing self-preservation or personal gain above all else can exacerbate crises and lead societies down dangerous paths.

While history contains both dark and inspirational examples, it is through these moments that societies grow, adapt, and, hopefully, become more attuned to the moral imperatives that shape our shared destiny. As we continue to face crisis after crisis, the moral choices made during these times are a testament to the complexity of self-preservation.

From its beginnings as a fundamental biological instinct to its current state as a multifaceted concept intertwined with ethics, self-preservation has shaped evolution and human history. As we continue to navigate the challenges of the modern world, understanding the intricate interplay between instinct, morality, and technology is essential.

RELATIONSHIP SELF-PRESERVATION

We must first analyze the significance of self-preservation in our lives before we can properly comprehend it in relationships. Maintaining and defending one's bodily, emotional, and mental health can be called self-preservation. In terms of partnerships, this idea entails establishing sound boundaries and prioritizing our needs to avoid putting our well-being at risk for the sake of a relationship.

Self-Preservation's Importance in Romantic Relationships

In all kinds of relationships, self-preservation is essential, but its significance in romantic partnerships cannot be stressed. When we start dating someone, we frequently discover that we are concerned about their pleasure and well-being, sometimes even putting their needs above ours. Any healthy relationship requires sacrifices, but it's critical to realize when we are giving too much of ourselves. Self-preservation becomes crucial in this situation for preserving a healthy partnership.

Self-Preservation's Function in Upholding Healthy Relationships

Giving and receiving in a relationship must be balanced, and each partner must respect and prioritize the needs of the other. But it's also crucial to put our needs first and keep a strong sense of self throughout the process. Neglecting our needs can make us bitter, exhausted, and dissatisfied in our relationships, creating an unhealthy dynamic.

Taking care of our physical, emotional, and mental health is crucial to self-preservation. Setting limits, expressing our wants, and partaking in enjoyable activities are all examples of how to do this. We can better present our best selves in the relationship when we put our own needs first.

It is crucial to understand that protecting oneself does not entail being egotistical or ignoring our partner's needs. Instead, it entails striking a healthy balance between our wants and the partnership's. We can give more to the relationship and develop a deeper, more satisfying connection with our spouse if we care for ourselves.

When You're Sacrificing Yourself in a Relationship and How to Recognize It

Self-awareness and reflection are necessary to identify when we are making excessive sacrifices in a relationship. Additional pointers on recognizing self-sacrifice are provided below:

Keep an eye on Your Emotions: Be aware of your emotional state in the connection. You may contribute more than you should if you frequently feel depleted, emotionally spent, or miserable.

Evaluate Your Priorities: Consider whether you've been putting your partner's needs and wants ahead of your own. Have you stopped engaging in your interests or hobbies or socializing with loved ones? If so, you might be forgoing your happiness to preserve the connection.

Consider your partner's honesty and openness while evaluating your communication patterns. You may be giving up your voice in the relationship if you find yourself avoiding conversations about your wants, worries, or boundaries.

Analyze Your Guilt Feelings: Pay attention to any guilt you experience when expressing your demands or wants. It's a common sign that you could be making too many sacrifices when you feel bad about prioritizing yourself.

Examine Justifications and Excuses: If you frequently justify your partner's actions or minimize problems in your relationship, it may be a sign that you are putting your well-being at risk to keep the peace or prevent conflict.

Ask for Advice from Reliable Friends: Occasionally, individuals closest to us can provide insightful commentary. Ask close friends or family members who are familiar with you about the dynamics of your relationships.

It's crucial to act to regain balance once you realize that you may be making too many sacrifices in the relationship:

Set Boundaries: Specify your boundaries in detail and let your spouse know what they are. Healthy limits let you keep your identity while being part of a marriage.

Set Self-Care as a Priority: Include self-care in your daily routine without exception. Prioritize what makes you happy and fulfilled, whether spending time on your hobbies, working out, or spending time with loved ones.

Establish open lines of communication with your partner about your needs and feelings. Mutual understanding and compromise are the foundation of a strong partnership.

Consider Professional Assistance: Consulting a therapist or counsellor for advice can be very helpful if the problems in your relationship are complex and difficult to manage on your own.

The first step in exercising self-preservation is realizing when you're giving too much in a relationship. Long-term pleasure and happiness depend on balancing looking after oneself and the partnership.

Setting Limits in Relationships to Support Your Self-Preservation

In relationships, maintaining one's self-respect requires establishing sound boundaries. Setting time and energy restrictions, being explicit about what we need, and rejecting conduct that goes against our beliefs are all examples of boundaries. Even though it might occasionally be awkward or challenging to set limits, doing so is essential to preserving a positive dynamic in the relationship.

Knowing when our limits have been crossed is crucial to setting boundaries. This can be challenging, particularly if we have a history of failing to set boundaries or are in a committed relationship with someone who frequently flouts them. However, it's crucial to be aware of when our boundaries have been crossed and to politely but firmly let the other person know.

Consistency in enforcing boundaries is a crucial component of setting them. Setting limits just once and then disregarding them is insufficient. For our boundaries to be effective, we must continuously communicate with one another and uphold them. Although it can be difficult, doing this is vital for both our happiness and the stability of the partnership.

The Rewards of Giving Your Own Needs Priority in a Relationship

When we put our needs first in a relationship, we safeguard our health and foster a more positive dynamic between our spouse and ourselves. We allow our partners to understand our point of view and work toward a mutually advantageous relationship when we are upfront about our requirements and set boundaries. Prioritizing our needs also helps us develop self-confidence and self-esteem, positively affecting every aspect of our lives.

It is crucial to understand that putting our needs first does not entail disregarding or being selfish about our partner's needs. It refers to striking a balance between our requirements and our spouse's. We can better be present in the relationship and fulfil our partner's needs when caring for ourselves. This leads to a more contented and enduring partnership in the long term.

How to Tell Your Partner About Your Needs for Self-Preservation

Effective self-preservation necessitates communication in a relationship and entails more than just what you say; it also involves timing and delivery. Here are some additional approaches to think about:

Select the Right Time: When speaking with your partner about crucial issues, timing is everything. In the middle of a conflict or other high-stress circumstances, refrain from bringing up the need for self-preservation. Choose a time when both of you are calm and can give the topic your full attention. A relaxed and encouraging atmosphere is necessary for effective communication.

Communication is not just about words; pay attention to nonverbal cues. Body language, tone of voice, and facial expressions are nonverbal cues that can reveal much information. Consider your and your partner's nonverbal cues when discussing your desire for self-preservation. To encourage a more open and receptive environment, maintain eye contact, speak calmly, and avoid defensive postures.

Use "I" Statements: Express your requirements using "I" statements rather than phrasing them as accusations or expressions of blame. Instead of saying, "You never help with anything around the house," try, "I feel overwhelmed when I have to manage all the household chores alone." "I" statements clear your demands and emotions without putting your partner on the defensive.

Active listening is essential for effective communication. It's important to carefully listen to your partner's point of view and express your requirements. Let your spouse finish their sentence without interjecting and express your appreciation for their feelings. This exhibits respect and fosters an atmosphere where you both feel comfortable talking about your requirements for self-preservation.

Avoid Making Judgments: When explaining your desire for self-preservation, avoid assumptions about your partner's motives or course of action. Instead of saying, "You always prioritize work over spending time with me," you may say, "I've noticed that we haven't spent much quality time together lately, and I miss that." This technique focuses on your feelings and experiences instead of making assumptions about your partner's intentions.

Express Boundaries Clearly: It's essential to set boundaries to protect yourself. Your partner has to know exactly what your expectations and boundaries are. Let your partner know that you need time alone to recharge, for instance, and explain why this boundary is important to you. Healthy boundaries aid in the reduction of misunderstandings and disputes.

Keep Your Options Open: Healthy partnerships frequently necessitate compromise. It's important to communicate your wants for self-preservation, but you should also be open to hearing what your spouse needs. Finding common ground and workable solutions helps improve communication and guarantee that each partner's demands are satisfied.

Use positive reinforcement by expressing your thankfulness and admiration when your partner complies with your self-preservation demands or responds positively to them. Positive reinforcement can promote a more harmonious relationship by motivating your partner to keep meeting your needs.

Self-preservation demands must be effectively communicated through what you say and when and how you express it. You can foster a supportive and understanding environment in your relationship by picking the right time, using "I" statements, paying attention to nonverbal cues, actively listening, avoiding judgments, clearly expressing boundaries, remaining open to compromise, and using positive reinforcement. This strengthens relationships and increases the possibility that partners will seek one another's needs.

Overcoming Fear and Guilt When Engaging in Relationship Self-Preservation.

It might be difficult to practice self-preservation in relationships, especially if we experience dread or shame. We could be concerned that establishing limits or putting our needs first will result in disagreements or a strained relationship. It's crucial to remember Changing our viewpoint, cultivating self-compassion, and getting help from dependable friends or experts may be necessary to overcome our anxiety and guilt.

Recognizing that we are not accountable for the feelings or responses of others can help us change our viewpoint when we are engaging in self-preservation in relationships. Although it is normal to wish to prevent confrontation or unfavourable reactions, it is not our place to control other people's feelings. Setting boundaries and prioritizing our needs allows us to take ownership of our health, which ultimately helps the relationship. In addition to helping us overcome our fears and guilt, practising self-compassion and getting support from close friends or experts can also boost our confidence to exercise self-preservation in relationships.

Keeping Yourself Alive While Maintaining Your Partner's Compassion and Empathy

Self-preservation is crucial, but balancing our and our partner's needs is also crucial. While compassion is expressing concern and caring for our partner's well-being, empathy entails understanding and connecting with our partner's feelings. In a relationship, demonstrating empathy and compassion can deepen the sense of trust and understanding between the partners.

It's crucial to remember, though, that compassion and empathy shouldn't come at the expense of our health. In a partnership, it's critical to establish boundaries and express our wants. Doing this ensures we aren't risking our mental and emotional well-being to protect our partners. A successful relationship requires striking a balance between self-preservation and empathy/compassion.

Frequently Held Myths Dispelled About Self-Preservation in Relationships

Self-preservation in relationships is the subject of numerous widespread myths and misconceptions. For instance, some people could think that establishing boundaries or putting our own needs first is disrespectful or self-centred. But in truth, self-preservation is necessary for a respectful and successful partnership. Some other common misconceptions include that expressing our demands would cause conflict or putting our personal needs first will harm our relationships. Debunking these myths is essential to successfully implementing self-preservation in relationships since they are untrue.

Another prevalent misconception regarding self-preservation in relationships is that it necessitates total independence from our spouse. That is untrue. Self-preservation entails caring for oneself and one's needs, but it doesn't preclude asking our spouse for assistance or support when necessary. In reality, expressing our demands and accepting assistance from our spouses can improve their bond.

Some might think that acting to protect ourselves requires us to be distant or watchful in our interpersonal interactions. This is untrue as well. Establishing boundaries and putting our needs first can promote more honest and open communication in a partnership. We are more inclined to be open and vulnerable with our partners when we feel confident in our abilities to meet our needs.

How to Improve Your Relationship by Using Self-Preservation Techniques

Self-preservation techniques ultimately create a stronger and more satisfying dynamic between partners in partnerships. We build trust and respect in the relationship when we put our needs first and are upfront about what we require. Setting clear boundaries, prioritizing our needs, and having open and honest conversations with our partners are all essential components of a good relationship built on self-preservation. It also entails cooperating to develop a relationship that will benefit both parties and demonstrating empathy and care for our partner.

Self-preservation in a relationship also entails being in charge of our feelings and not depending on our spouse to meet our demands. This may entail practising self-care techniques like exercise or meditation and, when necessary, asking friends or a therapist for assistance. We become better partners and can contribute more fully to the relationship when we care for ourselves. Ultimately, developing a great relationship through self-preservation necessitates striking a balance between putting our needs first while keeping our partner's needs in mind and cooperating to establish a positive and fulfilling dynamic.

Examining the Relationship between Self-Love and Self-Preservation

Self-care and self-preservation go hand in hand. By caring for our needs, we finally show self-love when we exercise self-preservation. Similarly, prioritizing self-love increases our propensity to protect ourselves in all spheres of life, including our relationships. Ultimately, developing a foundation of self-love and self-preservation in our relationships results in a greater sense of contentment and fulfilment in our lives.

It's crucial to remember that in a relationship, loving and protecting oneself does not entail being egotistical or disregarding the needs of our partners. It entails establishing sound boundaries, being clear about our needs and wants, and ensuring our well-being is not jeopardized. We can present as our best selves in our relationships and build more peaceful and satisfying partnerships when we practice self-love and self-preservation.

Trauma in Childhood and Adult Relationships: Effects on Self-Preservation

Trauma from childhood can have a significant effect on our capacity to practice self-preservation in interpersonal interactions. Traumatic events might cause an inability to set appropriate boundaries and emotions of unworthiness and abandonment anxiety. Understanding how childhood trauma affects adult relationships is essential to healing and learning to put our needs first. To work through these concerns, seeking support from a reputable therapist or counsellor can be beneficial.

It's crucial to remember that adult relationships can show different signs of childhood trauma in different ways. Some people could have trouble trusting others, while others might have trouble expressing their emotions. Healthy relationships can be challenging to establish and maintain due to these issues. On the other hand, it is feasible to get through these challenges and create gratifying connections with the correct assistance and resources.

In addition to consulting a professional, exercising self-compassion and self-care can aid in the recovery from childhood trauma. This can involve engaging in enjoyable and relaxing activities, establishing boundaries with others, and developing the awareness and ability to counteract negative self-talk. By putting our health first, we can break away from traumatizing patterns and create healthier and more satisfying relationships.

Understanding the Warning Signs of a Relationship That Endangers Your Ability to Preserve Yourself

Our well-being depends on our ability to spot warning indications of a connection that endangers our ability to protect ourselves. Warning flags may include feeling exhausted or unfulfilled in the relationship, being pressured to put our needs aside for the partnership's sake, and being the victim of manipulation or emotional abuse. If we become aware of these red flags, it may be necessary to reevaluate the relationship and put our own needs first.

In partnerships, self-preservation is crucial to preserving a positive, meaningful dynamic with our partners. We build trust and respect in the relationship by prioritizing our needs and establishing clear limits. Self-preservation demands a delicate balancing act between putting our needs first and demonstrating understanding and caring for our spouse. We can prioritize our well-being and create solid, satisfying relationships by recognizing the warning signs of an unhealthy relationship and asking for help when required.

It's crucial to understand that maintaining oneself in a relationship does not constitute selfishness. We must care for ourselves to present our best selves in the relationship. We are more equipped to offer and receive love healthily when we put our health first. For our spouse to comprehend and respect our demands and boundaries, it is equally crucial to express them properly. Doing this establishes a secure and encouraging environment for our spouse and ourselves.

SELF-PRESERVATION AND MENTAL HEALTH

People like you will encounter a variety of concerns and problems in today's fast-paced environment that could harm your mental health. Your mental stability will be damaged due to problems with your career, family, and relationships with your boyfriend or friends. But did you realize that maintaining mental health is crucial for independence? If you're unfamiliar with it but want to learn more, you've come to the correct place since we'll explain its significance.

Protecting your mental and emotional health is part of caring for yourself beyond spa days and Self-care Sundays. You can only give from the overflow when your cup is full. To help you put it into perspective, we've enlisted the expertise of the experts.

To defend oneself from harm or death is the definition of self-preservation. In the context of COVID-19, we've grown accustomed to exercising caution daily to safeguard our families and ourselves. According to life coach Sharon Piel, the past several months have been difficult, making taking care of yourself more crucial than ever. As a transformational coach, author, and international speaker, Justin Cohen notes, "It's about taking care of your emotional, social, and spiritual needs by managing stress, practising self-compassion, and staying connected to your loved ones." However, this shouldn't be at the price of another person. Instead, it ought to benefit both parties. Justin offers this real-world illustration. How can you practice self-preservation in various contexts, such as at work, home, or relationships? "The air steward urges you to take care of your oxygen mask before aiding others. "A doctor will advise you to exercise, eat five portions of fruit and vegetables, and sleep for seven to eight hours daily."

So, remember to maintain good physical, mental, and cognitive health. How empathetic and kind are you when upset, disappointed, or distressed? On the other hand, being ill impairs your ability to be creative, focused, and empathic. How do you know when to be selfish and when to prioritize your needs? To persuade someone into acting in a way that benefits you but not them, such as taking their money and offering nothing in return, is selfish. But suppose you decide to quit a relationship that isn't fulfilling you.

Even if it could be hurtful to the other person, according to Justin, it eventually benefits them since "if it's not working for you, sooner or later it's not going to work for them either," That's mutual self-preservation because it's a selfless deed that will ultimately serve the interests of both of you. Our experts concur that being non-selfish is the best form of self-care. "When we take care of ourselves, we can serve and care for others," asserts Sharon. 'You can't pour from an empty cup,' as the adage goes. She continues, "Stress and overwhelms weaken your immune system, making you more prone to sickness if you feel physically and emotionally spent. Self-care is essential for your wellness because it enables you to function at your best and present the finest version of yourself.

Self-care Techniques:

Physical

Get enough sleep and rest, have regular, healthy meals, drink lots of water, and exercise daily outside in the sunshine.

You may create a healthy living and working environment by eliminating clutter and toxic people.

Make time for enjoyable activities like hobbies, sports, or reading.

Emotional

Exercise (particularly yoga), journaling, mindfulness practices, and meditation are all beneficial techniques to manage stress.

Set limits, particularly if you work from home. The end of your working day should coincide with when you normally leave the office.

Social

Utilize a tool like Zoom or Skype to communicate with family and friends routinely.

Create a network of support. When you're down and in need of inspiration, it is beneficial.

Spiritual

Spend some time by yourself—preferably in nature—meditating or praying. Put your artistic or musical creativity on display.

Things You Should Quit Telling Yourself to Improve Your Mental Health

Your mind serves as an editor. Choosing how to tell the tale of what occurs to you every day is one of its jobs. It dictates how every encounter and disaster fits into your life's story. Your brain's interpretation of events like a dispute with a partner or a bad job interview can eventually determine whether or not you feel bad or have self-defeating thoughts.

Your editorial brain is tempted to take shortcuts to protect yourself when feeling nervous or stressed out. The "must" filter is one such shortcut. Musts are the ideas we hold about how the world ought to function and conduct ourselves in it. Your brain wants to fit every occurrence into these cute little boxes, but these "musts" are frequently inaccurate or illogical. They disregard the nuanced aspects of the human condition in favour of absolutes. Here are a few "musts" to be on the lookout for when you start to worry. Stop telling yourself these five musts, and see how your mental health improves.

1. I must Always Have Everyone's Love.

The expectation of complete and unqualified acceptance underlies a lot of self-defeating ideas and actions. Although it is immensely normal to want acceptance, love, and admiration, you start to lose your sense of self when you repeatedly alter your behaviour to fulfil this want. You change swiftly to fit other people's perceptions, becoming a chameleon. Your attention is on everyone else, making it impossible to recall what is significant to you. You relate compliments, or Facebook likes to your sense of worth.

The truth is that you can't always make everyone happy. This "must" is both reckless and irrational. Try concentrating on your values instead. What conduct fosters regard for oneself? Instead of just looking for their affection, how can you be helpful to others? What form of peer recognition is useful, and what is pure vanity?

2. I have to Succeed In Everything.

Fear and anxiety can be sparked by setting oneself up for perfection in every action. Additionally, when you have unrealistic expectations for yourself, procrastination is more likely to occur. The most successful people frequently experience multiple failures and accept their imperfections. Consider how your life can be complete despite and because of your limits rather than letting perfectionism paralyze you.

Be careful not to generalize when you fail to combat this "must." It's not necessarily true that you won't ever find work if you don't get the job interview. You won't spend the rest of your life alone with 70 cats if you get stood up on a date. You may tell you're in unreasonable land when your brain starts using terms like "always" and "never" automatically.

3. Things I Worry About Must Be Upsetting Me.

Today's world makes it simple to worry incessantly, especially with the availability of social media and 24-hour news channels. You become trapped in the belief that you are placing yourself in danger when you let down your guard or give attention to something else. But obsessing is not the same as looking into it. Examining the nature and reality of your concerns will frequently reveal that you have two options: face them or accept that they are inevitable. Acceptance does not imply submission; rather, it implies putting more emphasis on the things you can control than the things you cannot. Even though the cosmos will eventually die from heat, you can recycle your rubbish.

4. I Must Stay Out Of Any Disputes.

It could seem safer to cut off or distance yourself from challenging people. We can avoid experiencing such unpleasant and dirty feelings when anxiety decreases. But this is just a band-aid solution. When you always go for the quickest exit, you'll feel increased emotional reactivity and self-defeating thoughts in your head.

All of us will run into people in life with whom we disagree. There will be arguments, miscommunications, and stress related to communication. It can initially appear impossible to disagree head-on while attempting to comprehend. But communication is a skill that must be developed to live a more tranquil and ultimately happier life. Long-term, you will be less bothered by interpersonal drama if you learn to be deliberate and expressive under pressure and in uncertain situations.

5. I Must Be In Charge Of Everything.

Having solid control over your life is not a bad quality. Those who feel more in control of their inner selves are more likely to be tougher when faced with difficulties in life. However, when this expectation permeates every circumstance and event, it turns into a deadly "must."

Your life's events are mostly the result of chance. While we can't forecast the future completely, we shouldn't retreat to our beds and remain inactive. Instead, think about how you can remain positive and strong regardless of the outcome of the dice. You'll bounce back from bad situations quicker and feel less guilty and self-blame.

The first step in challenging your brain's editorial process is a straightforward investigation. Consider which of these "musts" applies when you practice writing your ideas and expectations about a scenario. Ironically, having more control over your emotions and reactions comes from accepting difficult and unpredictable moments. It's remarkable how much more interesting life gets when you accept the complexities of your humanity and the world around you.

The Value of Self-Preservation and the Need for Mental Health Care

Whatever you are going through right now, it would be beneficial if you understood the concept of self-preservation and how crucial it is to maintain your mental stability. You will undoubtedly feel motivated when you realize how crucial it is to protect your health.

Better mental health allows you to act exactly and without hesitation, which is beneficial for protecting oneself. You can gather and conserve your energy to meet every task that comes your way correctly if you emphasize taking care of yourself more than anything else.

You may easily achieve your goals while being motivated positively if you protect yourself better against danger or damage from outside factors. Additionally, you can be free from several conditions that harm your mental health, such as stress, sadness, etc. As we previously stated, taking care of or protecting yourself will enable you to keep a good mental state, which will benefit your entire life.

With a positive mindset, you'll be inspired to try new and different things, accomplish things you previously believed were impossible for you, take on new challenges, and be bold rather than fearful. By protecting your mental health, you may effortlessly access your potential skills, enhancing your strength and ability to perform any task.

The Effects of Not Taking Care of Your Mental Health

You understand how crucial self-preservation is, so let's look at the effects of neglecting your mental health. If you don't have a good mentality, you'll run into many issues, and it will be devastating if your mental health is out of whack. Let's examine the negative consequences of disregarding your mental wellness.

Did you realize that your physical and mental health are interrelated? Whether you are aware of it or not, having a mental illness will also negatively impact your physical health. Some of these include cardiovascular illnesses, hypertension, etc. Additionally, if your mental health is poor, it's possible that your immune system won't work effectively.

Additionally, you will experience diminished productivity if you do not prioritize fueling your mental health. It might be challenging for someone who experiences mental health problems like anxiety, stress, or depression to be active and pay attention to the daily chores assigned to them.

Additionally, you will never succeed in sustaining relationships, participating in society, or enjoying life. Your life's quality will consequently suffer. As a result, you need to set aside some time to take care of yourself to avoid these problems.

When their mental health is poor, many people occasionally become hooked on various substances and other illicit activities. It will be difficult for someone hooked on drugs, alcohol, or any other illegal substance to escape and end this vicious cycle. Therefore, you should be extra cautious and take care of your mental health before becoming hooked; otherwise, it would be too late.

When your mental health is poor, one of the main problems you may experience is a variety of mental illnesses or disorders, including depression, anxiety, stress, etc. These are the most typical mental health conditions you will experience. When you have one of these mental health conditions, you'll feel helpless and isolated and have a pessimistic outlook. Therefore, it is preferable to maintain good mental health while concentrating on it rather than allowing these problems to affect you.

Techniques for Self-Preservation

You can practice self-preservation in a variety of ways without allowing various negative thoughts to impact your outlook negatively. Maintaining mental health will be simple once you are familiar with these techniques.

Exercise, meditation, and other self-care practices are the first steps you should take to protect yourself. You can calm your mind and lessen tension by exercising or meditating while surrounded by beautiful scenery, like nature.

Setting boundaries or constraints for yourself in everything you do is the next thing you should do to protect yourself without affecting your mentality. For instance, you should set boundaries at work or in your relationship. Even if anything happens that tears your heart while you do this, your attitude won't be harmed.

You can ask friends, family, or specialists for assistance if you experience various mental disorders. By doing this, you'll experience less stress or other mental health problems and be able to regain your mental health.

Self-Compassion Training for Better Mental Health

Our mental health affects all our lives, from our relationships and employment to our physical health and general happiness. It is a vital part of our entire well-being. Unfortunately, millions of people worldwide are suffering from conditions including stress, anxiety, depression, and other mental health problems. In this environment, it is essential to investigate practical methods for enhancing mental health, and cultivating self-compassion is one such method.

Treating oneself kindly and sympathetically, particularly during adversity or pain, is known as self-compassion. It entails treating oneself with the same compassion and empathy that one would show a struggling friend. Research has increasingly demonstrated that self-compassion is essential for improving mental health and overall well-being. In this essay, we will examine the idea of self-compassion, consider its advantages, and discuss how to nurture it to enhance mental health.

Knowing One's Compassion

Self-compassion is a concept that has acquired popularity in modern psychology, especially as a result of the work of Dr. Kristin Neff. Buddhist teachings primarily influence it. It is made up of three main parts:

Self-kindness is the practice of treating oneself with the same warmth and consideration as one would a good friend. Self-kindness requires acknowledging one's pain and responding with empathy and understanding instead of harsh self-criticism and self-judgment.

Another crucial component of self-compassion is understanding that suffering is a shared human experience. People who are compassionate toward themselves know that everyone experiences pain and difficulties to varied degrees. As a result, they don't feel isolated or alone in their hardships.

Being mindful is noticing one's thoughts, feelings, and experiences objectively. It entails admitting one's suffering and unpleasant feelings in a non-reactive, non-judgmental way in the framework of self-compassion. Instead of repressing or avoiding their suffering, people who practice mindfulness learn to stay present with it.

Self-Compassion's Positive Effects on Mental Health

Numerous research have shown how self-compassion has a good effect on mental health. Here are several major advantages:

Self-compassion has been associated with a decrease in how stressful and anxious people consider themselves to be. The excessive stress and anxiety frequently linked to self-criticism and self-judgment are less likely to occur when people address their suffering with love and empathy.

Self-compassion enables people to manage their emotions more skillfully, which leads to improved emotional control. They can stop unpleasant emotions from getting out of hand by being aware of their feelings and responding with self-kindness. Those prone to mood disorders benefit most from this enhanced emotional management.

Enhanced self-esteem: Self-compassion is linked to a better level of self-esteem, even though this may appear paradoxical. Self-compassion promotes a healthier self-image by recognizing that everyone makes errors and has setbacks, in contrast to self-criticism, which can diminish self-worth.

Better relationships: People who are self-compassionate are frequently more compassionate toward others. While people learn to be kind to themselves, they become more empathic and understanding while interacting with friends, family, and coworkers. This may result in increased social support and more amicable relationships.

Self-compassion protects against the negative consequences of life's trials, increasing resilience. People with high self-compassion are more resilient and stronger to overcome challenges.

How to Develop Self-Compassion

After exploring the significance of self-compassion for mental health, let's talk about some useful techniques for cultivating it:

Embrace self-compassionate self-talk by paying attention to it. Replace your self-critical or judgmental thoughts with self-compassionate ones whenever you notice yourself doing so. Think of a close friend going through a similar predicament and speak the same kind and compassionate words to them.

The cultivation of self-compassion can be cultivated through mindfulness meditation.

Practice non-judgmental awareness of your thoughts and emotions while meditating on your breathing. Approaching negative thoughts with self-kindness and acknowledging that suffering is a part of the human experience will help you overcome them.

Self-compassion activities: There are particular exercises and guided meditations to increase self-compassion. Writing letters to oneself, using self-compassionate affirmations, or imagining a compassionate presence are common exercises in this category.

Seek professional assistance: If you experience difficulties with self-compassion or have pervasive problems with self-worth and self-esteem, you might consider counselling. A qualified therapist can offer direction and support as you progress toward better mental health.

Practice self-care: Self-care practices like getting adequate sleep, eating healthily, exercising frequently, and engaging in hobbies you enjoy can help you feel more compassionate toward yourself. These actions serve as a reminder to yourself that you are deserving of love and care.

Accept imperfection: Recognize that perfection is an impossibility. Accept your flaws and errors as opportunities for improvement. Consider these failures as opportunities for learning rather than self-criticism.

Connect with others by talking about your challenges with dependable friends or in support groups.

The understanding that others experience comparable difficulties might strengthen the sense of shared humanity essential to self-compassion.

Set reasonable goals: Make adjustments to your expectations to reflect reality.

Self-criticism can flourish in the presence of perfectionism and unattainable objectives. Set attainable objectives and acknowledge any progress, no matter how tiny.

Practice self-forgiveness for past transgressions and regrets. Self-compassion can be hampered by harbouring guilt and shame. Keep in mind that being human means making mistakes.

Keep a self-compassion notebook: Keep a journal where you frequently record incidents of self-compassion, such as when you were nice to or supported yourself. Thinking back on these occasions can help reinforce self-compassionate actions.

Challenges in Self-Compassion Development

It is not always simple to practice self-compassion, even though it has enormous benefits for mental health. Many people encounter several obstacles on their path to self-compassion:

Influences from culture and society: The pursuit of perfection and self-criticism are frequently encouraged in society. Adopting self-compassion as a value can be difficult because cultural norms and media portrayals can reinforce unattainable standards.

Inner critic: The inner critic, or that internal voice of condemnation and self-criticism, can be deeply ingrained and resistant to change. Rewiring these mental habits requires time and effort.

Some people are concerned that self-compassion may result in self-indulgence or laziness. Self-compassion does not imply neglecting obligations or delaying personal development; rather, it promotes a more positive outlook for dealing with difficulties.

Fear of exposure: Being self-compassionate frequently entails admitting vulnerability and accepting flaws. This may be unsettling for people who have learned to repress their feelings or present an image of invulnerability.

Self-compassion cultivation is an effective strategy for enhancing mental health and general well-being. It entails being nice to oneself, appreciating the humanity of others who are suffering, and engaging in mindfulness exercises. The advantages of self-compassion include reduced stress and anxiety, higher emotional control, improved self-esteem, better relationships, and more resilience.

Self-compassion is a skill that can be learned and strengthened through practice, even though it may be difficult to cultivate. People can develop a stronger feeling of self-compassion by altering their negative self-talk, doing self-compassion exercises, getting professional treatment when necessary, and embracing self-care.

Self-compassion improves emotional well-being and resilience in a world with rising mental health problems. It serves as a reminder that we deserve the same courtesy and compassion that we so freely provide to others. In addition to enhancing our mental health, practising self-compassion helps build a sympathetic and kind culture.

SELF-PRESERVATION IN DIFFERENT ENVIRONMENTS

Understanding the basic survival instincts that guide human behaviour is crucial before going into the specifics of self-preservation in various contexts. These impulses, commonly called the "four F's" — fighting, fleeing, feeding, and mating – are the building blocks of self-preservation.

Fighting: Human biology is firmly ingrained with the urge to protect oneself from immediate threats. When faced with danger, our bodies release adrenaline, preparing us for physical confrontation. This instinct has played a significant part in our evolutionary history, enabling our ancestors to survive confrontations with predators and other perils.

Fleeing: When fighting is not an option or the threat is overpowering, the impulse to flee or escape kicks in. Humans are endowed with the ability to perceive danger and make rapid decisions about whether to face or flee it. This instinct has helped human survival by allowing us to avoid life-threatening situations.

Feeding: To ensure survival, humans must receive food. The drive to seek food and nourishment is a crucial part of self-preservation. This instinct helped our early ancestors create the behaviors of hunting and gathering, which still impacts our nutritional preferences and eating patterns today.

Mating: Humans are inclined to mate, which motivates them to look for mates and participate in procreative activities. Reproduction is necessary for the survival of the species. This instinct is responsible for developing social ties and relationships, which in turn aid in an individual's and their offspring's survival and wellbeing.

Nature's Self-Preservation Mechanisms

Outdoor Survival

Self-preservation in natural settings like forests, deserts, and jungles frequently involves fighting, running, and gathering resources. Adaptability, resourcefulness, and awareness of the local ecosystem are essential for wilderness survival.

Fighting: In the wild, conflicts over territory with other animals or with predators can set off the fighting drive. People may use tools and weapons like spears or knives to defend themselves and ensure survival. Another self-preservation weapon is fire, which can fend off predators and offer warmth and illumination.

Running: Running becomes the main survival tactic when faced with overwhelming hazards like enormous animals or natural calamities. In natural settings, humans must be able to navigate across challenging terrain, locate safety, and flee from peril.

Resource acquisition: In the wild, finding food and water is essential. Foraging, fishing, and hunting are common methods of obtaining food. Understanding how to track animals and use traps is crucial for those living in natural settings.

Polar Survival

Self-preservation faces unusual difficulties in the harsh, forgiving Arctic climate. Specialized survival techniques are needed due to the intense temperature, scarcity of food sources, and isolation.

Insulation and Shelter: Arctic residents must prioritize remaining warm and dry to prevent hypothermia. Maintaining body temperature requires insulating materials such as clothes, igloos, and other types of shelter. Self-preservation in this setting frequently entails preserving energy and limiting exposure to the elements.

Food and Water: The lack of available food requires effective hunting and fishing techniques in the Arctic. For instance, Inuit people have created inventive methods for obtaining fish, seals, and whales. Common activities include ice fishing and putting out traps for terrestrial animals. Another crucial activity is melting ice for drinking water.

Community and cooperation are essential in the Arctic, where existence frequently depends on cooperation within small, close-knit groups. The collective self-preservation of the group depends on sharing resources and information. Individuals can survive the harsh surroundings and isolation of the Arctic thanks to group effort.

Urban Environments and Self-Preservation

City Survival

Self-preservation takes on a new shape in the huge concrete jungles of cities. Less immediate predator threats and more complicated cultural forces and lifestyle considerations are the problems confronted.

Security and safety: People who live in cities place a particular emphasis on personal protection. Instead of fighting off predators physically, they have to deal with crime, car accidents, and the possibility of getting hurt in heavily populated regions. In the city, self-preservation frequently entails vigilance and using security tools like locks and alarms.

Economic Survival: In metropolitan settings, maintaining a stable economy is essential for preserving oneself.

People must find jobs, manage their money, and plan for the future to ensure their well-being. It becomes essential to pursue education and career progress to survive.

Access to Resources: Urban locations provide access to various resources, including social services, healthcare, and education. Having access to these resources becomes essential to maintaining oneself. Making one's needs heard and navigating bureaucratic systems become crucial survival skills.

Living in Large Cities

Megacities provide particular difficulties for self-preservation due to their large populations and few resources. The proximity of people and infrastructure can cause competition for scarce resources and enhance disaster susceptibility.

Resource management: Survival in megacities depends on effective resource management. This entails finding inexpensive housing, controlling the food and water supply, and addressing problems like waste management and pollution. The welfare of individuals and communities depends on the effective use of resources.

Megacities are frequently vulnerable to natural disasters and other emergencies. People must be ready to flee or seek refuge in earthquakes, floods, or other disasters. Plans for dealing with disasters must include communication and evacuation procedures if people are to survive.

Community Resilience: In megacities, creating resilient communities is essential. Neighborhood associations and grassroots organizations frequently play a vital role in preparing for and responding to disasters. In the face of significant obstacles, inhabitants' chances of survival can be improved by cooperation.

Self-Preservation and Cultural Factors

Understanding that cultural and personal traits influence self-preservation tactics and environmental influences is crucial. Cultural norms, assumptions, and values shape individuals' perceptions of and reactions to dangers and difficulties.

societal norms

Cultural standards may govern how people act on their impulses for self-preservation. Individual autonomy and self-reliance may be emphasized in some cultures, while collectivism and group assistance may be more important. These cultural norms impact whether people are more prone to rely on their resources or ask for help from others.

Values and Beliefs

Beliefs in religion and philosophy can have an impact on self-defence techniques. For instance, people with religious roots may turn to prayer and faith-based activities under difficult circumstances.

Secular people, on the other hand, can concentrate on logical problem-solving and looking for workable answers.

Identified Personal Qualities

Character factors, including risk tolerance, adaptability, and resilience, greatly influence self-preservation. Some people may be more inclined to take chances naturally than others, who may be more cautious and risk-averse. In various contexts, these personality qualities affect how people make decisions.

A fundamental feature of human nature, self-preservation takes several forms depending on the surroundings. Humans use various techniques to secure their survival and well-being, whether in wild environments with several immediate physical risks or urban landscapes with numerous complicated socioeconomic difficulties. Cultural elements, human traits, and the particular requirements of each context influence these tactics.

It is crucial to comprehend how self-preservation functions in various situations to meet the changing difficulties of the modern world. It emphasizes the value of flexibility and the demand for a comprehensive education, readiness, and community resilience strategy. Self-preservation is ultimately a powerful force that defines our behaviour and how we interact with the world, making it a constant source of intrigue and research.

Self-Preservation In Workplace

In the workplace, self-preservation involves understanding and setting healthy boundaries. This includes knowing one's rights and responsibilities and asserting personal limits and expectations. Conflict resolution skills are also essential in maintaining positive relationships with colleagues and superiors. Conflict is inevitable in any work environment, but how it is addressed can significantly affect the overall atmosphere and productivity. By developing effective conflict resolution skills, individuals can navigate disagreements and disputes constructively and respectfully. This involves actively listening to others, seeking common ground, and finding mutually beneficial solutions. By addressing conflicts head-on and finding resolution, individuals can protect their emotional well-being and contribute to a harmonious work environment.

In today's digital age, self-preservation in online spaces is becoming increasingly important. Cybersecurity measures, such as using strong passwords, enabling two-factor authentication, and being cautious of phishing attempts, can help safeguard personal information and prevent identity theft. It is also vital to be careful of online content and to exercise responsible digital citizenship. By being aware of potential online threats and proactively protecting oneself, individuals can maintain their privacy and security in the virtual world.

During emergencies, self-preservation entails being prepared and having the required abilities and resources to face unexpected situations. Emergency preparedness includes having a well-stocked emergency kit with vital supplies, such as food, water, and first aid equipment. It also requires making an emergency plan and familiarizing oneself with evacuation routes and emergency contacts. This entails evaluating potential risks and hazards in the workplace, such as fire or natural disasters, and devising a plan of action to minimize these risks. This strategy may involve designing evacuation routes, identifying assembly sites, and ensuring that emergency exits are well-marked and accessible. Additionally, it is vital to familiarize oneself with emergency contacts, such as the authorized safety officer or emergency services, so that that help may be swiftly and efficiently contacted in an emergency. By taking these proactive measures, individuals can enhance their safety and contribute to a safer work environment.

Self-preservation also extends to intimate connections. It is crucial to surround oneself with helpful and trustworthy folks who contribute positively to one's life. Building a strong social network of friends and loved ones can provide emotional support and a sense of belonging. However, it is equally vital to be discerning in picking friends and acquaintances, as not all connections may be healthy or helpful. Awareness of red signals and setting boundaries might help protect oneself from toxic or abusive relationships.

Conducting extensive background checks, checking references, and clearly articulating expectations can assist in ensuring the safety and well-being of both people engaged. Putting personal security and safety first is critical when bringing others into one's private or work area.

Self-preservation in various settings refers to tactics and routines safeguarding one's physical, psychological, and emotional well-being. Individuals can improve their personal safety and general quality of life by comprehending the instinct of self-preservation, learning physical self-defence tactics, preserving mental and emotional well-being, and putting strategies into practice in varied contexts.

FINANCIAL SELF-PRESERVATION

Financial self-preservation is a fundamental and continuously applicable feature of personal finance that transcends space and time. In an increasingly complicated and dynamic environment, it encompasses the art and the science of protecting one's financial security, possessions, and future. The fundamental goal of financial self-preservation is to safeguard oneself. One's loved ones from financial vulnerabilities and to ensure a secure financial future, even though the specifics of these tactics can vary from person to person and even from generation to generation.

The idea of financial self-preservation has gained increased significance in today's fast-paced and unpredictable economic environment. Economic downturns, unforeseen medical emergencies, the nature of employment and technology, and other factors all highlight the importance of taking a thorough and proactive approach to managing one's finances. This introduction lays the groundwork for a more in-depth investigation of financial self-preservation and its application to everyday life.

What Financial Self-Preservation Is All About

Financial self-preservation is fundamentally about taking charge of one's financial future despite outside influences and market instability. It stands for a dedication to ensuring one's financial security, protecting against unforeseen misfortunes, and making plans for a safe and wealthy future.

Financial self-preservation involves more than just building wealth or succeeding financially; it also involves developing financial resilience. It is the material counterpart to the ingrained human survival instincts. People must take proactive steps to safeguard their financial security from unforeseen hazards, just as they naturally try to protect themselves and their loved ones in dangerous situations.

Getting Around in an Uncertain World

Financial unpredictability is a major concern in the modern world. The 2008 global financial crisis highlights the need for financial self-preservation, the COVID-19 pandemic's economic effects, and the omnipresent threat of unforeseen life occurrences. It serves as a barrier against the unknowable, a safety net against financial shocks, and a way to become resilient in the face of difficulty.

It recognizes that life is uncertain and that financial security is not a given financial self-preservation. It implores people to be ready for unforeseen circumstances that can upset their financial equilibrium. Financial security and peace of mind include making informed decisions regarding budgeting, saving, investing, and debt management.

The Essential Elements of Financial Self-Preservation

Each crucial element that makes up financial self-preservation plays a crucial part in accomplishing the ultimate goal of financial security. These essential elements comprise:

An emergency fund is the cornerstone of financial self-preservation for unforeseen costs like medical bills, auto repairs, or job loss. It guarantees that people won't rely on high-interest debt during tough times.

Budgeting and Expense Control: An effective budget enables people to manage their money wisely, allocate funds to necessary costs, and pinpoint areas where savings can be made.

Debt management: Prudent debt management prioritizes repaying high-interest debt and can keep the weight of debt from threatening financial stability.

Insurance is essential for reducing the financial burden of unforeseen catastrophes. Some insurance products include health, life, disability, and property insurance. They offer a safety net to shield assets and offer money when needed.

Investment and Wealth Preservation: When preparing for retirement, diversification of portfolios, risk management, and wealth preservation-focused investment strategies are essential.

Financial self-preservation includes estate planning, which involves using wills, trusts, and beneficiary designations to ensure that one's assets are dispersed as intended and reduce potential tax liabilities.

In a world where financial security can be elusive, financial self-preservation is not a luxury but a need. It is a proactive strategy for safeguarding one's financial security, defending against unforeseen catastrophes, and laying the groundwork for a secure and wealthy future.

In the following pages, we will examine techniques, best practices, and helpful hints for putting these principles into reality daily as we go deeper into each aspect of financial self-preservation. The information provided will equip you to take charge of your financial future and successfully manage the obstacles of a constantly shifting financial world, whether you are just starting on your financial path or looking to strengthen your current financial security.

Self-Preservation Financial Principles

The cornerstone of a stable and resilient financial future is financial self-preservation. It entails collecting essential ideas and tactics people can use to maintain financial security and prepare for unforeseen difficulties. Learning and implementing these concepts can create a strong foundation for financial security and mental tranquillity. We will examine the essential principles of financial self-preservation in this part.

Emergency Reserve:

Creating an emergency fund is among the most important components of financial self-preservation. This fund acts as a safety net for money, offering a buffer for unanticipated costs or emergencies like medical bills, car repairs, or job loss. According to financial experts, a minimum of three to six months' worth of living expenditures should be saved in this fund. It guarantees that people won't have to rely on high-interest debt or sell investments during a crisis, which contributes to maintaining financial stability.

Budgeting and Cost-Cutting:

Effective planning is necessary for efficient money management. Individuals who create and follow a budget can better evaluate their income and expenses, allot resources to necessary needs, and spot areas where they may make savings. Budgeting helps people better manage their daily expenditures and frees up money for investments and savings, which promotes long-term financial stability.

Management of Debt

A crucial aspect of maintaining one's financial stability is managing debt. Credit card debt, for example, has a high-interest rate and can swiftly undermine financial security. People should prioritize paying off high-interest debt and refrain from taking on additional obligations. Consolidation, negotiating with creditors, and creating a structured repayment plan are all possible debt management tactics.

Insurance Protection:

Insurance is critical in maintaining financial stability by reducing the financial burden of unanticipated events. While life insurance safeguards heirs if a breadwinner dies, health insurance covers medical costs. Property insurance protects against loss or damage to possessions, while disability insurance can restore missed wages resulting from illness or injury. Protecting one's financial security requires evaluating insurance requirements and ensuring they are met.

Investing and Preserving Wealth:

Long-term financial self-preservation requires investment methods that prioritize wealth preservation. Investment portfolio diversification across several asset classes and risk categories can reduce losses during market downturns. Risk management techniques can shield assets from substantial losses, such as placing stop-loss orders or hiring a financial counsellor. Regular portfolio assessments and consistent retirement account contributions are crucial to preserve wealth.

Estate Management:

An often overlooked component of financial self-preservation is estate planning. It entails developing a plan to distribute assets after death to ensure that one's intentions are carried out, and prospective tax liabilities are kept to a minimum. Estate preparation is incomplete without wills, trusts, and beneficiary designations on bank accounts and life insurance policies. Proper estate planning can safeguard family assets and enable a smooth wealth transfer to heirs.

Individuals can take charge of their financial future and develop resilience in the face of unforeseen setbacks by adopting these principles of financial self-preservation. These guidelines offer a road map for handling money, safeguarding property, and planning for a safe and prosperous future. Incorporating these foundations into your financial strategy is a proactive step toward financial well-being and peace of mind, regardless of whether you are just beginning your financial journey or looking to strengthen your current financial security.

Maintaining Your Financial Well-Being During Economic Uncertainty

The Great Depression and the more recent worldwide recession brought on by the COVID-19 epidemic are just two examples of the many financial crises and economic downturns throughout history. The significance of protecting one's financial security becomes even more clear during these unsettling times. This essay highlights the need for proactive financial planning and steps to create resilience as it investigates the ideas and techniques of financial self-preservation in the face of economic uncertainty.

Knowledge of Economic Uncertainty

Unpredictability or instability in economic conditions is referred to as economic uncertainty. It can appear in various ways, such as volatile stock markets, shifts in the labour market, inflation, and economic downturns. The financial lives of individuals can be significantly impacted by such uncertainty, making it crucial to implement financial self-preservation techniques that can withstand economic downturns.

The Importance Of Maintaining One's Finances

Financial self-preservation refers to guidelines and tactics for safeguarding one's financial security regardless of the state of the external economy. It is more important to be ready for economic changes than to try to forecast them. Building financial resilience is the key objective since it enables people to survive economic shocks and keep their financial stability.

Budgeting and Cost-Cutting

Effective budgeting is one of the first and most important measures in maintaining financial stability during economic volatility. Making a thorough plan that breaks down your income, expenses, and savings objectives is part of budgeting. Here's how to go about it:

Analyze Your Financial Situation: Start by assessing your present financial situation. Your income, fixed expenses (such as rent or a mortgage, utilities), variable spending (like groceries and entertainment), and debts must all be calculated.

Establish a priority list for your critical costs, such as your rent or mortgage, food, medical care, and insurance premiums. Your budget should include a considerable amount for these.

Spending less on non-essential items is prudent, given the current economic climate. Review your discretionary spending, including entertainment, subscriptions, and eating out, and consider reducing or eliminating wasteful costs.

Budget a percentage of your income to create or maintain an emergency fund. This reserve can serve as a financial safety net during rocky times and can be used to pay unforeseen costs.

Regular Monitoring: Monitor your spending plan and make any adjustments. Being adaptable and flexible is essential for maintaining one's financial stability.

Both Job Security And Income Protection

Job security becomes a serious worry during uncertain economic times. Consider the following tactics to protect your financial stability:

Improve Your Skills: Invest in ongoing education and skill development to stay current in your industry or look into alternative career options.

Establish and sustain a professional network through networking. You can access employment prospects and learn about market trends by making connections.

Diversify your income streams by having several sources of income. Part-time jobs, side jobs, and freelance work can add to your financial security.

Prepare an emergency plan in case you lose your work. This could entail scaling back on non-essential spending, moving temporarily, or downsizing.

Investment Techniques for Risky Markets

In times of economic instability, prudent investing is essential to maintaining financial security. Consider the following investment tactics:

Spread your investments among various asset types (stocks, bonds, and real estate) to diversify your portfolio and lower your risk. Diversifying can protect your portfolio from suffering significant losses in one industry.

Risk management: Be aware of your comfort level with risk and modify your investing portfolio as necessary. During uncertain times, conservative investing may seem more enticing.

Regular Monitoring: Keep abreast of economic and market indicators. Consider working with a financial advisor to ensure your investments align with your financial objectives.

Long-Term Perspective: Refrain from rash investing choices in response to momentary market changes. You can withstand economic turbulence by adopting a long-term investment approach.

Investment-Specific Emergency Fund: If you invest, you might want to keep an investment-specific emergency fund on hand. Doing this allows you to avoid selling investments at disadvantageous times to cover crises.

Management of Debt During Economic Recessions

Having a lot of debt during an uncertain economy can make things worse. It's crucial to manage debt effectively:

Pay Off High-Interest Debt First: Pay off high-interest loans like credit card accounts. Your financial stability can be quickly eroded by high-interest debt.

Talk to your creditors about temporary relief alternatives, such as lower interest rates or deferred payments, if you're having trouble making debt payments.

Avoid taking on new debt: Be cautious when taking on new debts like loans or credit cards during uncertain times. Consider whether you need to take on more debt.

Emergency Debt Relief Options: Remember that certain government initiatives or financial entities may provide debt relief during recessions. These initiatives might offer short-term financial relief.

Getting Ready for Recovery

The state of economic uncertainty is not always present. Just as crucial as managing uncertainty is preparing for recovery. Here's how to set yourself up for financial development when the economy picks up:

Rebuilding Savings: Reestablish your long-term savings and emergency fund after stabilizing the economy.

Investing in Education and Skills: To improve your professional possibilities, consider investing in educational or training programs. Increasing your skill set can improve your employment prospects and financial standing.

Long-Term Financial Planning: Review your long-term financial goals and plans during stable times. Make necessary adjustments to your strategy and keep accumulating riches.

Financial self-preservation involves actively managing your financial resources to face challenges and maintain stability during economic uncertainty rather than trying to forecast or control economic events. You may develop financial resilience that will serve you well in difficult and prosperous times by creating an effective budget, safeguarding your income, choosing intelligent investments, managing debt responsibly, and preparing for economic recovery. Adopting these tactics enables people to control their financial futures, deal with economic uncertainty, and eventually guarantee a better financial future.

Strategies for Wealth Preservation After Your Life

All high-net-worth families require professional wealth management to identify their wealth preservation methods. "Ultra-high net worth" families are those whose investable assets are valued at over $30 million, although even these families are not considered to have "ultra-high net worth." Click here to read our guidance on increasing and safeguarding your family's wealth if you are a high-net-worth individual with more than $10 million in investable assets.

You occasionally read about inspiring people who have accumulated substantial money. Such people frequently combine ambition with courage, hard work, and unwavering consistency in their mission. In today's fiercely competitive world, becoming "High Net Worth" is challenging, but becoming "Ultra-High Net Worth" is an even harder - and rarer - feat.

At Pillar Wealth Management, we offer high-net-worth families with $5 million to $500 million in liquid assets a full range of wealth management services. Click here to schedule a free consultation and learn more about wealth preservation techniques if you are unhappy with your existing investment manager.

Growing your wealth requires working with the proper wealth manager. Even while it would require exceptionally high levels of carelessness or a significant financial catastrophe for someone with this much wealth to experience financial problems like foreclosure or bankruptcy, it is not unheard of.

Riches to Rags stories have been in the news recently, particularly during the financial crisis of 2007, when many families went from having "Ultra-High Net Worth" to only having "High Net Worth" or even going bankrupt!

UHNW families have a completely different set of financial issues than the average person. They do not typically have to deal with issues like failing to pay their rent or having trouble keeping up with their car payments.

UHNW families need to make wise financial planning decisions based on strong wealth preservation strategies to successfully maintain a high standard of living and sustain their wealth across several generations.

These choices include making the most of investment vehicles, properly preparing an estate, and dealing with efficiently changing tax laws.

1. Full-Scale Financial Planning

You need above-average financial planning if you have above-average assets. UHNW families have a more extensive range of difficulties to cope with than 'regular' families because their financial situation is more complicated.

The ideal wealth preservation tactics need handling greater taxes, a larger financial portfolio, several properties, and keeping track of your charitable endeavours.

Effective management of these factors is made possible by thorough financial planning, enabling you to create family wealth protection and growth strategies. Unlike conventional financial planning, this form surpasses typical income estimates and retirement funds. It includes every aspect of your financial affairs.

These consist of:

- Controlling finances and debt
- investment strategy
- Taxes
- Retirement preparation
- estate preparation
- management of risk
- Generally, comprehensive financial planning consists of the following steps:
- A thorough discussion of your values and aspirations for your family and yourself
- Creating a financial projection based on your present financial situation
- obtaining professional guidance and formulating wealth preservation plans
- forecasting your financial situation in light of their suggestions
- a well-defined strategy
- Click here to speak with one of our wealth managers and learn more about comprehensive financial planning.

2. Gathering Your Assets

UHNW individuals and families frequently open up some form of investment account with numerous financial institutions to diversify their wealth. They think that this is a successful strategy for lowering risk.

Diversification is more about how your money is invested than where it is held.

Setting up numerous identical investment accounts can work against you by making it much harder to maintain track of your money rather than in favour of diversifying your investment.

There are numerous additional benefits to consolidating your assets with a single trustworthy advisor who will suggest the appropriate wealth preservation techniques you should consider. These are the causes:

Lower Costs: Opening investment accounts with different financial institutions will probably result in greater costs for you.

Streamlined Administration: Keeping track of your investments is simpler with fewer tax filings and account statements.

No Duplication of Investments and Efforts: Since two advisors' efforts are rarely coordinated, there is a significant likelihood of duplication of investments (i.e., less diversity) and efforts.

Simplified Estate Settlements: Having a single point of contact makes things simpler for your executor.

Easier and More Efficient Retirement Planning: When your adviser has a greater grasp of your numerous income streams, it is easier for them to develop an effective strategy for maximizing your retirement income.

3. Teaching Your Children Financial Responsibility

Even though substantial money must be earned over a long period, it can all be lost in a flash.

Self-made people understand the actual worth of money since they worked long and hard to accumulate their fortune. However, they might not share this fundamental value because their children and grandchildren were raised more wealthy.

Teach your children the value of fiscal responsibility if you want your money to last for several generations. You can benefit from a variety of wealth preservation measures in this regard.

The first entails giving your kids a fair allowance and directing them to divide it among charitable contributions, savings, and spending. This fosters financial responsibility in kids and teaches them the value of money while fostering social responsibility.

Among other wealth preservation techniques, one successful technique is creating a monthly budget accommodating realistic costs and family activities. If your kids ask you for something that costs more than you have planned, tell them you'll think about it next month.

4. Using Extra Resources Efficiently

The majority of UHNW people and families have extra money. Here are some practical wealth protection techniques to safeguard accumulated assets.

Give the assets to low-income family members as a possible present. If the family member is a minor, their lower tax rate will be applied to the taxes assessed on capital gains. But since you will be considered the dividend and interest income source, you will be liable for paying their taxes. If they are considered legal adults, they must pay taxes on the income from the asset; however, they will do so at a much-reduced rate.

Consider investing the money in a tax-free life insurance policy if you ever need insurance. By doing this, you can avoid paying taxes on their revenue. Following the distribution of your estate, the income will be distributed as a tax-free benefit to the policy's beneficiaries.

Another approach to avoid paying capital gains tax on surplus assets is to donate appreciated publicly traded shares to recognized charities.

Click here to read our advice if you need assistance locating a financial advisor who can manage surplus assets by implementing the most effective wealth preservation techniques.

5. Management of Risk

Effective risk management is essential in the mix of wealth preservation techniques since it is essential to safeguarding your hard-earned cash. Because they weren't ready for dangers like lawsuits and market instability, many ultra-high-net-worth families have lost large chunks of their fortune in the past.

Liability insurance is one approach to secure the protection of your assets in case of a lawsuit.

Risk of Market Volatility: Diversifying your investments is the best defence against the threat of market volatility. UHNW families can lower risk by choosing the route of tax-free bonds and diversifying investments by geographic area, industry, and class.

Risk of Income Loss: Serious illnesses and impairments are regrettably a fact of life and can affect anyone. Your family can be safeguarded from long-term or transient income loss by purchasing long-term care and critical sickness insurance.

Keep in mind that risk management is essential for financial stability. You must make a few adjustments to prepare for various investment risks and attain financial stability by implementing the correct wealth preservation techniques.

6. Donating To Charities

You can maximize the impact of your charitable donations by utilizing a variety of wealth-preservation tactics, including the following:

As previously indicated, publicly traded shares that have increased in value after being donated to an approved charitable organization are not subject to capital gains tax. The receipt you receive also shows the market value of the securities you gave.

Consider establishing a charity foundation if you wish to leave a lasting charitable legacy. A public foundation might be better for you if you don't desire daily involvement, even though a private foundation will give you more flexibility and control.

7. Wills and Trusts

In your will, you can also establish testamentary trusts. Your beneficiaries will receive income tax benefits from it that they wouldn't receive from an outright inheritance.

The revenue earned will be added to their regular income and taxed appropriately in the event of an outright inheritance. This can raise their tax rate and lower their payment after taxes.

Testamentary trusts have other advantages than potential tax advantages. You can even set things up such that a disabled relative or a child from a previous marriage receives their inheritance. Consequently, be sure to include them in your wealth preservation strategy.

Sharing the Income Of A Family With A Very High Net Worth

Splitting the income is another practical method for UHNW families to lower their tax obligations.

Why? The American tax system, as you may know, dictates that the more money you make, the more money you owe in taxes.

Families might potentially save thousands of dollars in taxes by distributing the family's income among its members, particularly to low-income ones.

If you go this route, you must consult a financial advisor with experience creating wealth preservation programs.

8. Creating A Business Succession Plan

Here are a few successful business succession wealth preservation measures if you intend to pass your company on to your children or grandchildren:

Determine which children have the skills and desire to run your company. Decide who will succeed you, and then gradually involve that individual in corporate decisions after you've made your choice. Introduce them to key business contacts and gradually transition them into a position of responsibility. This transition should last five to ten years.

Have a financial strategy that includes individual pension plans, an estate freeze to reduce taxes, and insurance to protect you from risks and unplanned events. Moreover, provide a shareholder's agreement.

9. Property Planning for Vacation

When an ultra-high-net-worth family is involved, owning a vacation home can lead to several problems. Passing the property on to the next generation without causing a fight is one of the main concerns. However, with some careful planning, you can not only amicably transfer the property but also lower taxes.

Listed below are some sensible methods for wealth preservation:

An effective option to leave your children a vacation home is through an inter vivos family trust. You can put off future capital gains tax and avoid probate tax.

A co-ownership agreement can be made to lay out the ground rules if two or more kids own the property.

Creating Wealth vs. Protecting It

How to Make Money

It would help if you had a strategy, namely a financial plan, to build wealth. A financial plan provides the framework for building wealth.

A financial plan specifies how your assets will be diversified and includes an asset management strategy based on your income objectives and risk tolerance. Many alternatives include stocks and bonds, mutual funds, bank accounts, CDs, ETFs, etc.

A retirement and savings plan are both parts of a financial plan. It might set up some budgeting and debt management planning.

The continuous monitoring of your investments should be part of your plan because your objectives will change as the market does.

How to Maintain Wealth

Maintaining wealth requires proper money management, including asset diversification, continual risk and investment monitoring, keeping a cash reserve for emergencies, and obtaining insurance.

Your asset portfolio may need to vary over time to reflect changes in your financial demands and aspirations. The market will change; therefore, it's critical to be informed of new investing opportunities and seize them when they present themselves.

As changes occur in your financial circumstances, reevaluate your risk profile. You might discover that you wish to move into more predictable assets or that you can handle more risk. Please track your finances to ensure they can handle any unforeseen situations. You should have enough money to pay for your living expenses for up to six months. As you age, you might want more money to cover healthcare costs.

Examine your insurance contracts. Check to see if they offer enough protection, such as a life insurance plan that will care for your beneficiaries' needs.

The distinctions between wealth generation and wealth preservation

Any action that enhances your money is known as wealth creation, such as making new investments and seeing them appreciate. However, you protect your wealth if your assets don't include risk, like those in a savings account. Additionally, building wealth entails keeping your assets' worth from declining over time. As a result, wealth growth and preservation are related.

Through asset diversification and risk control, you must strike a balance between the two.

SELF-PRESERVATION IN HEALTH AND WELLNESS

Maintaining physical health, fostering mental and emotional well-being, and using preventative healthcare practices are all included in the issue of self-preservation in health and wellness. It is essential to emphasize self-care and use measures that protect our general well-being in today's fast-paced, stressful world.

Exercise is one of the essential elements of self-preservation in health and fitness. Our bodies and minds can benefit greatly from regular exercise. It helps to strengthen bones and muscles, as well as to increase flexibility and endurance. Endorphins, naturally occurring mood enhancers, are also released during exercise and can aid with anxiety and depression symptoms. Exercise can also help you sleep better, think more clearly, and lower your chance of developing chronic illnesses like heart disease, diabetes, and cancer.

It's critical to establish specific goals when it comes to fitness. Whether your goal is to maintain general fitness, lose weight, gain muscle, increase flexibility, or all of the above, having clear goals can help you stay motivated. It is advisable to speak with a medical practitioner or a licensed personal trainer to develop a customized exercise program appropriate to your unique requirements and capabilities. They can help you choose the best training frequency, intensity levels, and exercise varieties.

Example: Absolutely! Here is a five-day-a-week exercise schedule.

Strength training on Day 1

- Perform light exercise for 5 to 10 minutes to warm up, such as jumping jacks or running.
- Carry out the following exercises for three sets of 8–12 repetitions:
- Weighted squats
- exercise bench
- sagging rows
- Bench press
- Bench presses
- Trench dips
- Finish by stretching for 10 minutes.

Cardiovascular Exercise on Day 2

- Pick your chosen aerobic exercise, swimming, cycling, or running.
- Set a goal of 30-45 minutes of moderate to vigorous cardio.
- Don't forget to perform 5–10 minutes of easy cardio as a warm-up and cool-down.

Day 3: Active Recovery or Rest

- Skip a day of vigorous exercise and switch to low-impact exercises like yoga or strolling.

Day 4 High-Intensity Interval Training (HIIT)

- Perform gentle cardio for 5 to 10 minutes to warm up.
- Carry out four to five rounds of the following exercises:
- Burpees
- Rock climbers

- Squat jumps
- Push-ups
- Plank
- Each exercise should be conducted for 30 seconds, followed by a 10-second break.
- Finish by stretching for 10 minutes.

Day 5: Core and Flexibility Training

- Perform gentle cardio for the first 5–10 minutes.
- Focus on exercises that enhance flexibility and core strength, such as:

1. Yoga positions (such as the child's pose, warrior poses, and downward dogs)

2. Pilates movements, such as variants of the plank and leg circles

- Set out 30 to 45 minutes for core and flexibility exercises.
- Stretch for 10 minutes to wind down.

Always pay attention to your body's signals and change the workouts' duration or intensity as necessary. A healthcare practitioner should always be consulted before beginning any new workout program.

Nutrition is essential for self-preservation in terms of health and wellness in addition to exercise. A well-balanced diet of various nutrient-rich foods is crucial for maintaining ideal physical and mental health. To conserve biological functioning and supply energy, it's critical to eat a variety of carbohydrates, proteins, healthy fats, vitamins, and minerals. A diet rich in fruits, vegetables, whole grains, lean meats, and healthy fats can lower your chance of developing chronic diseases and help prevent nutrient deficiencies.

Ultimate System for Long-Term Loss of Weight!

Join the thousands of happy customers who used our ground-breaking Sunshine in a Bag Shake to reach their weight loss objectives. Fad diets are over; welcome to a healthier, happier you. Our method is made to fit into your hectic lifestyle with ease. With our delectable smoothie, you may skip two meals and have a prudent, wholesome meal for the third. One shake and some fruit can be blended to create two meals suitable for breakfast, lunch, or dinner. The best thing, though? Real success stories like Robin Martinez's 267-pound weight loss in our program support our system. When can you begin your transformation? Join us on the path to a healthy you by consulting your doctor!"

Daily Meal Plan for Weight Loss

• **Breakfast Shake:** For a nutritious and satisfying breakfast, combine 1 scoop of protein powder with 1 cup of unsweetened almond milk, 1/2 banana, and 1/2 cup of frozen berries.

You may make a nutrient-dense lunch shake by blending 1 scoop of protein powder with 1 cup of unsweetened almond milk, 1/2 an avocado, 1 small cucumber, 1/2 a lime, and a handful of spinach or kale.

- Snack: If you're hungry between meals, munch on almonds or cherry tomatoes.

- Dinner: Eat a balanced meal with lots of vegetables and lean protein; examples are salads with grilled chicken, salmon with roasted vegetables, stir-fries with tofu, and loads of vegetables.

- Evening Shake: If you feel like having a shake in the evening, mix 1 scoop of protein powder with 1 cup of unsweetened almond milk and some frozen fruit. This can help satisfy any sweet cravings without jeopardizing your weight loss goals. Remember to drink lots of water and avoid sugary drinks like soda to support your weight loss goals better!

Survival of the Body

Physical self-preservation, which includes a variety of behaviours and practices aimed at preventing sickness, extending life, and improving physical functioning, is centred on preserving and protecting the body's health and vitality.

Food Intake and Diet

A balanced and nutritious diet provides the body with the essential nutrients, vitamins, and minerals required for optimal functioning and is the cornerstone of physical self-preservation. A diet high in fruits, vegetables, lean proteins, and whole grains supports general health and helps prevent chronic diseases.

Physical Activity And Exercise

Regular physical activity is essential for maintaining and enhancing physical well-being because it strengthens muscles, develops flexibility, improves cardiovascular health, helps manage weight, and elevates mood by releasing endorphins.

Sleep and Rest

The body repairs and rejuvenates tissues, consolidates memories, and regulates hormones while we sleep. Chronic sleep deprivation can lead to various health issues, including impaired cognitive function and an increased risk of chronic diseases. Adequate rest and quality sleep are essential for physical self-preservation.

Hydration

Dehydration can result in exhaustion, dizziness, and cognitive impairment. Water is necessary for digestion, circulation, temperature control, and the elimination of waste products. Maintaining appropriate hydration is crucial to physical well-being.

Prevention-Based Medicine

A proactive approach to physical self-preservation, routine medical exams, screenings, and immunizations enable early identification of potential health disorders and facilitate prompt interventions.

Stress Reduction

Stress management practices, such as mindfulness meditation, yoga, or relaxation exercises, are crucial for maintaining physical well-being because chronic stress can harm physical health.

Protecting One's Mental And Emotional Health

Mental and emotional self-preservation aims to protect and nurture one's psychological and emotional well-being. It entails methods for dealing with stress and emotions and ways to keep one's mind sharp and resilient.

Emotional Intelligence

Emotional self-preservation requires self-awareness, which entails recognizing and comprehending one's emotions to manage them properly.

Stress Management Methods

Deep breathing, progressive muscle relaxation, and guided imagery are among the techniques that can lower stress and improve emotional well-being.

Psychology and Therapy

A safe environment to examine and resolve emotional difficulties is provided through counselling or therapy, which can help manage and preserve mental and emotional health.

Social Networking

Maintaining healthy social relationships is crucial for emotional well-being because they offer emotional support, lessen feelings of loneliness, and boost general happiness.

Building Resilience

Resilience is the ability to bounce back from adversity and adapt to life's obstacles, and it can be developed. Building resilience may involve establishing a growth mindset and building problem-solving abilities.

Meditation and mindfulness

Individuals can improve their emotional stability, reduce worry, and stay present with the support of mindfulness techniques like meditation and mindfulness-based stress reduction.

Physical and Mental Health In Balance

Achieving a balance between the two is critical for total wellness. Physical well-being can have a substantial impact on mental health and vice versa. Recognizing the interdependence of physical and mental health is crucial for comprehensive self-preservation.

The Brain-Gut Connection

Healthy gut flora can favourably influence mood and cognitive function, highlighting the relevance of a balanced diet in mental self-preservation. Emerging research reveals a close relationship between the gut and the brain, known as the "gut-brain axis."

Health Mental Exercise

In addition to its positive effects on physical health, regular exercise significantly impacts mental health. It can reduce anxiety and depressive symptoms, improve cognitive function, and raise self-esteem.

Slumber and Emotional Control

Lack of sleep can cause mood swings, impatience, and an increased susceptibility to stress. Quality sleep is essential for emotional self-preservation.

Physical Health and Stress

Managing stress is crucial for physical and mental self-preservation, as chronic stress can physically appear as immune system malfunction, cardiovascular problems, and digestive disorders.

Lifestyle and Environmental Factors

Environmental and lifestyle factors greatly influence self-preservation in health and wellness, and individual decisions about their surroundings and daily routines can substantially impact their well-being.

Toxins in the Environment

Physical self-preservation requires minimizing exposure to environmental toxins, such as pollution and hazardous chemicals and may entail selecting clean and sustainable living conditions.

Balanced Integration Of Work And Life

Prolonged stress from overworking can significantly affect physical and mental health, so finding a healthy work-life balance is essential to general self-preservation.

Use of Technology

Establishing digital boundaries can be a safeguard. Mindful use of technology is crucial for emotional self-preservation. Overuse of screens and social media can cause tension and worry.

Outdoor Activities and Nature

Nature exposure is linked to lower stress levels and better mood, so spending time outside and participating in outdoor activities can have a restorative effect on both physical and mental well-being.

Comprehensive self-preservation requires understanding the interplay between physical and mental health, and environmental and lifestyle factors play a role.

It is a recognition of the intrinsic value of one's well-being and the active pursuit of practices and habits that support a fulfilling and vibrant life. By adopting this holistic approach to self-preservation, individuals can thrive in life's challenges and savor the richness of a healthy and balanced existence.

Promoting mental and emotional well-being is another crucial component of self-preservation in health and wellness. Stress management methods, such as mindfulness meditation, deep breathing exercises, and partaking in hobbies or activities that bring joy and relaxation, can help reduce stress and improve overall mental health.

SOCIAL NETWORKS AND THE COMMUNITY

In a world where interconnectedness and social bonds play a crucial role in individual and collective flourishing, understanding how self-preservation operates within these networks is essential. This essay explores the dynamics of self-preservation in community and social contexts.

Self-Preservation in Social Networks and Its Nature

This dynamic is deeply rooted in our evolutionary history, where the survival of early human communities depended on cooperation, mutual support, and collective defence against external threats. Self-preservation within social networks involves the instinctual drive to safeguard one's well-being while contributing to the well-being of the group or community to which one belongs.

Self-preservation in social networks today takes many different forms and operates on numerous levels in the complex and interconnected world we live in:

Individual Self-Preservation: At its core, individual self-preservation within social networks entails making choices and decisions that safeguard one's physical, emotional, and psychological well-being, including asking for help and support from one's social connections when confronting personal difficulties or adversity.

Individuals recognize that their well-being is intertwined with the group's well-being and actively work to strengthen the community's resilience and cohesion. Collective Well-Being: Simultaneously, self-preservation within social networks involves making contributions to the collective well-being of the community or group.

Interconnectedness: The concept of self-preservation in social networks emphasizes that maintaining and developing the community's resources and resilience ultimately helps each member individually. It recognizes the interconnectedness of people within a community.

Strengthening and Developing Relationships

Connections with family, friends, neighbours, and community members are at the core of self-preservation within social networks. Building and sustaining these relationships is fundamental to maintaining individual and communal well-being. Here are some major aspects:

Relationships are built on effective communication and connection, so it's important to participate in conversations actively, listen with empathy, and show concern and care for others.

Mutual Support: Mutual support is what makes social networks successful. Giving support when required, whether emotional support during trying times or practical assistance during emergencies, builds reciprocity and trust.

Being trustworthy and reliable in one's commitments and promises strengthens the sense of security within a community. Trust is the cornerstone of self-preservation within social networks.

The ability to settle problems constructively and amicably rather than allowing them to fester is essential for maintaining happy relationships. Problems will inevitably arise in any social network.

Empathy and Understanding: In social networks, empathy and understanding are crucial elements of self-preservation because they help people recognize the distinctive experiences and viewpoints of others, which prevents misunderstandings and disputes.

Strength in Communities and Resilience

A resilient community can better overcome challenges and adversities, whether economic, environmental, or social. Here's how resilience is fostered in social networks:

Sharing of Resources: Sharing resources, whether tangible assets like food and shelter during a crisis or intangible resources like knowledge and skills, strengthens the community's resilience and is a common strategy for self-preservation within social networks.

Problem Solving and Innovation: Communities that prioritize self-preservation stimulate problem-solving and innovation. They collaboratively investigate solutions to obstacles, adapt to changing conditions, and develop new techniques for resilience.

Preparedness and Planning: Being proactive in preparedness and planning is a hallmark of community self-preservation. Communities generally build contingency plans for emergencies, ensuring they can respond successfully to unforeseen circumstances.

Social Capital: Social networks are a sort of social capital—a valuable resource that can be deployed in times of need. Building social capital through relationships and connections increases a community's ability to protect itself.

Crisis Response and Recovery: When crises or disasters occur, the strength of self-preservation within social networks becomes visible.

Communities that provide relief, support, and resources to impacted people display resilience.

Encouragement of a Sense of Belonging

A sense of belonging is a basic human need essential to self-preservation in social networks because it increases the drive to safeguard and preserve the group and its members. Here are some ways to foster a sense of belonging:

Diversity provides a stronger feeling of community, while inclusivity creates a sense of belonging for all members, regardless of their backgrounds, identities, or differences.

Shared Values and Purpose: When community members have similar values and a sense of direction, it strengthens their sense of community and drives them to work together for self-preservation.

Celebrating Traditions and Culture: Maintaining and honouring local customs, traditions, and cultural activities helps strengthen a sense of identification and belonging.

Encourage active participation and engagement in community affairs and decision-making processes to give people a sense of ownership over the well-being of their neighbourhood.

Communities frequently create formal and informal support networks, such as neighbourhood associations or neighbourhood clubs, where members can interact, exchange experiences, and collaborate to achieve shared objectives.

Self-Preservation Obstacles And Threats In Social Networks

Several risks and problems can hamper individual and collective well-being within communities, even though self-preservation within social networks is powerful.

Social isolation and loneliness can destroy a sense of belonging within a group and thwart attempts at self-preservation.

Internal conflicts or divides within a community might reduce its resilience and jeopardize efforts to preserve the group.

Resource shortage can weaken interpersonal ties and a community's ability to withstand environmental or economic distress.

External Threats: Communities may experience external threats, such as a drop in the economy, a natural disaster, or a public health emergency, which put their ability to defend themselves to the test.

Cultural Erosion: A community's identity and belonging can be weakened by the loss of cultural traditions and practices.

Leadership's Function in Self-Preservation

Effective leaders recognize the value of nurturing relationships, encouraging resilience, and creating a sense of belonging among their constituents; this is how leadership contributes to self-preservation in social networks and communities.

Strong leadership creates a clear vision and direction for the group or social network, which can motivate people to actively engage in self-preservation activities and cooperate to achieve common objectives.

Empowerment: By including community members in decision-making processes and motivating them to take charge of self-preservation activities, leaders empower their followers, who are more inclined to take the initiative to safeguard their community's well-being.

Effective conflict resolution prevents divisions and maintains the cohesiveness required for self-preservation. Skilled leaders are adept at resolving issues within the community or network.

Resource Mobilization: Leaders frequently have the power to mobilize resources, whether they be financial, material, or human, and they can use these resources to increase the resilience and ability of the community to survive on their own.

Leadership: Leaders can represent their community's interests and needs as advocates, making sure that they are taken into account at higher levels of government or in larger societal situations.

Leadership Challenges and Strategies

Effective leaders must manage these difficulties and put these well-being-promoting techniques into practice in order to lead in self-preservation within social networks and communities.

Diversity and Inclusivity: Diversity increases a community's capacity for self-preservation; leaders must ensure that all members of the community feel included and appreciated, regardless of their backgrounds or identities.

Conflict Resolution: Resolving conflicts among community members can be difficult. Therefore leaders need to be adept at doing so. They also need to be able to promote amity and understanding.

Long-Term Vision: Effective leaders should be able to strike a balance between the present needs of their community and the preservation of resources and future resilience.

Adaptability: Leaders must be able to change with the times and respond to new problems; they must be receptive to fresh perspectives and methods that advance self-preservation.

Leaders should engage in honest and open communication with community members to keep them informed and active in self-preservation activities. Communication is a cornerstone of leadership.

The Effects of Social Media and Technology

The terrain of self-preservation within social networks and groups has changed in the modern day due to social media and technology, which present both opportunities and difficulties:

Increased Connectivity: Social media and technology enable increased connectivity among community members, facilitating better communication, resource sharing, and self-preservation effort coordination.

Information Dissemination: Social media platforms make it possible for information to spread quickly during catastrophes, enabling communities to react more skillfully to disasters.

Building Communities: Social networks and online communities give like-minded people a way to interact and work together on self-defence projects.

Privacy Issues: The digital age also brings privacy and data security issues, making it important to safeguard personal data and uphold confidence in online communities.

Digital divide: Disparities in self-preservation capacities might result from unequal access to technology and the internet in different populations.

Case Studies for Community Survival

The concept of self-preservation within communities and social networks is shown by a number of real-world examples:

Urban communities frequently create community gardens where residents cultivate produce together. These gardens encourage self-sufficiency, generate a sense of belonging, and boost resilience by providing access to fresh produce.

Volunteer Networks: These networks show the effectiveness of collective action in self-preservation by providing assistance during catastrophes like natural disasters or health crises.

Neighbourhood Watch Programs: By watching out for one another, citizens maintain a sense of safety in their neighbourhoods through neighbourhood watch programs, which serve as an example of how communities may work together to improve safety and security.

Online support groups: The value of virtual communities in promoting self-preservation is highlighted by online support groups for people dealing with comparable issues, whether they be connected to health concerns, caregiving, or personal growth.

Self-Preservation's Vital Role in Social Networks and Communities

Nurturing relationships, fostering resilience, and embracing diversity are essential for self-preservation within social networks and communities. It reflects the deep-rooted human instinct to protect and support one another. Self-preservation within social networks and communities is an intricate interplay of individual well-being, collective resilience, and a shared sense of belonging.

Leaders encourage, advocate for, and mobilize resources to increase the community's capacity for self-preservation, essential for directing collective efforts and tackling difficulties within these networks.

Technology and social media have altered the digital age's self-preservation environment, presenting benefits and problems by facilitating connectivity, knowledge sharing, and community building but also requiring careful consideration of privacy and inclusion.

The effectiveness of group action and community support in self-preservation efforts, from community gardens to volunteer networks, is demonstrated by real-world case studies.

Self-preservation within social networks and communities ultimately reminds us that our interconnectedness and collective efforts are powerful tools for preserving the well-being of individuals and communities alike and is a testament to the strength of human bonds and the capacity of communities to thrive and flourish in the face of challenges.

SELF-PRESERVATION IN PERSONAL DEVELOPMENT

Self-preservation in personal development is a topic that explores many methods and approaches for developing oneself. It includes various techniques and ideas designed to improve one's general well-being and realize individual objectives.

Setting goals is one part of self-preservation in personal development. A sense of direction and purpose in life can be found in setting objectives. It enables people to pinpoint their goals and design a plan to help them realize them. People can stay motivated and focused on their growth journey by creating specific, attainable goals. Setting goals gives people a structure to organize their behaviours and choose a course of action consistent with their long-term objectives. They can stay on course and avoid becoming sidetracked by temptations or barriers that are just temporary. When people have a specific objective, they may divide it into smaller, more manageable tasks, making monitoring progress and recognizing accomplishments simpler.

Setting goals aids in maintaining motivation. When they have a clear goal to strive for, it offers them motivation to overcome obstacles and a sense of purpose. When they meet milestones, it gives them a sense of success and motivates them to keep going.

Setting goals enables people to assess their progress and make necessary modifications. By assessing their objectives regularly, companies may determine what is working and what needs to be changed. Individuals who reflect on their behaviour are better equipped to maintain accountability and advance personal development. A crucial component of self-preservation in personal development is setting goals. It gives them a sense of purpose, inspiration, and focus.

Another essential component of self-preservation in personal development is overcoming difficulties. The ability to overcome obstacles and challenges that come with life is crucial for personal development. This topic examines a variety of problem-solving techniques, resilience-building techniques, and other methods for overcoming challenges. It underlines the value of tenacity and tenacity in the face of difficulty.

One of the most important aspects of self-preservation in personal growth is developing positive habits and mindsets. Our everyday life and general well-being are greatly shaped by our habits. This subject dives into methods for creating good habits, like self-reflection, mindfulness, and gratitude exercises. It emphasizes the importance of positive thinking and its positive effects on self-improvement and personal development.

Self-care's significance in personal development is emphasized by self-preservation. The key to personal well-being is taking good care of oneself physically, psychologically, and emotionally. This article examines numerous self-care techniques, including physical activity, a healthy diet, enough sleep, and stress reduction. It underlines the significance of prioritizing self-care to maintain a balanced and healthy way of living.

In terms of personal development, self-preservation refers to various methods and tactics meant to promote improvement and personal growth. It entails prioritizing self-care, setting objectives, overcoming challenges, and developing a good attitude. Individuals can attain their personal goals, overcome obstacles, and lead meaningful lives by actively engaging in these disciplines.

THE ROLE OF SELF-PRESERVATION IN JUDGMENT

Self-preservation is a crucial factor in decision-making, frequently impacting our choices and behaviours. This essay explores the complex interplay between self-preservation and decision-making, analyzing how our innate survival mechanisms influence our decision-making and the cognitive mechanisms at work.

The Biological Need to Survive

All living things have a strong biological tendency toward self-preservation. It is the consequence of millions of years of evolution, during which time animals with strong systems for self-preservation had a higher chance of surviving and transferring their genes to succeeding generations. Various manifestations of this basic desire can be seen in the animal realm.

The fight-or-flight response occurs in both humans and many animals in the presence of a threat. This instinctive physiological response gets the body ready to either combat the threat or run away from it. Stress hormones are released, the heart rate rises, and awareness levels are raised.

Reflexes: Reflexes happen nearly instantly, without conscious thought, such as blinking when something is near the eye or removing one's hand from a burning object. They are made to shield people from harm and guarantee quick self-preservation.

Pain Sensation: The experience of pain is a potent deterrent against dangerous behaviour. For example, touching a hot stove immediately causes a withdrawal reaction to stop burn injuries.

Hunger and Thirst: By meeting their fundamental physiological demands, organisms are driven by biological signals like hunger and thirst to seek food and water. This ensures their survival.

Self-Preservation's Effect on Decision Making

Self-preservation instincts are most prominent while facing acute physical dangers, but they also influence our choices in subtler ways:

Risk aversion: When it comes to making judgments that could endanger their safety, evolution has benefited people who are cautious and risk-averse. For instance, people frequently hesitate to engage in risky activities or take on major financial risks.

The preservation of social and emotional ties is essential for human survival and has been true for a very long time. As a result, choices that improve interpersonal relationships and emotional health are frequently given priority. This encompasses decisions on interpersonal relationships, societal standing, and psychological safety.

Health and Longevity: The need for self-preservation has a strong influence on decisions regarding health behaviours, such as nutrition, exercise, and healthcare options. People frequently choose habits that increase their physical health and longevity.

Future Planning: Human decision-making is characterized by our capacity to foresee potential dangers and demands in the future.

Investing, saving money, and retirement planning are a few ways we can secure our well-being and get ready for challenges in the future.

Moral and ethical choices: Self-preservation impulses and ethical considerations frequently overlap. Morally sound choices can strengthen social bonds and teamwork, which in turn increase a community's chances of surviving.

Emotional biases and the Rational Brain

Although instincts for self-preservation are essential for existence, they may result in erroneous judgment. This is due to the fact that our brains have two distinct systems—a rational, cognitive system and an emotional, intuitive system—each of which has advantages and disadvantages of its own:

Emotional Biases: The emotional system has the potential to introduce bias into judgment. For instance, loss aversion (fear of loss) might cause people to act irrationally by keeping lost investments rather than selling them off.

Humans have a tendency to exaggerate some hazards while underestimating others when it comes to risk perception. This bias in risk perception may have an impact on choices. For instance, even if driving a car is riskier, some people may be more afraid of flying in an aeroplane, which is statistically safer.

Immediate gratification: Often, the urge for immediate gratification takes precedence over thinking about the long-term effects. This may result in rash choices that put immediate benefits ahead of long-term self-preservation.

Confirmation Bias: It's human nature for people to look for evidence that supports their current opinions and judgments. By limiting exposure to different viewpoints and evidence, this confirmation bias can impair rational decision-making.

Self-Preservation and Reasonable Decision-Making in Balance

It might be challenging to strike a balance between instincts for self-preservation and logical thinking. Self-preservation instincts have evolved to be helpful to us in many circumstances, but they can also result in unfavourable outcomes when biases and emotions are present. The following are methods for striking that balance:

Emotional Intelligence: Having emotional intelligence enables people to identify when their emotions are having an impact on their decisions. Meditation and other mindfulness exercises can be beneficial in this regard.

Encourage cognitive reflection by taking a step back and thoroughly weighing the advantages and disadvantages of a choice. Determine if your decisions are consistent with your long-term objectives and core beliefs.

Seek Diverse Perspectives: Be proactive in your search for different viewpoints and data sources. This prevents confirmation bias and ensures a more balanced approach to decision-making.

Consider consulting experts or getting professional help when making difficult or important decisions. Experts can offer insightful advice and lessen the effects of cognitive biases.

Practice Delayed Gratification: Teach yourself to postpone your desires and to think about the long-term effects of your decisions.

This can be especially helpful when making financial and medical decisions.

Danger reduction: Rather than relying primarily on emotional assessments of danger, take into account the larger context and mathematical probability when assessing risks.

Make ethical choices that are consistent with your values and advance your well-being and the welfare of others. Ethical decisions frequently produce more amiable and long-lasting results.

The Development of Self-Preservation and Decision-Making

It's crucial to understand the evolutionary roots of decision-making and self-preservation in order to fully appreciate the complex link between these two processes. The decisions taken by our predecessors throughout the history of our species were frequently a matter of life or death, and those who were skilled at self-preservation were more likely to pass on their genes.

Early Survival Instincts: In the early phases of human evolution, predators and unfavourable environmental conditions were only two of the many physical hazards that our ancestors had to deal with. The requirement to find food, shelter, and safety from imminent threats strongly influenced decision-making. For survival, it was essential to be able to swiftly identify threats and take appropriate action.

Social Evolution: As humans progressed, cooperation and social ties became more and more important for survival. The scope of decision-making increased to take group dynamics, trust, and cooperation into account. Altruism and reciprocal behaviour have become tools for increasing group survival.

Cognitive Development: As humans evolved, advanced cognitive abilities like reasoning, problem-solving, and planning also emerged. These cognitive skills allowed our ancestors to make difficult choices regarding resource allocation, resource allocation, and hunting.

Complex Societal Decisions: As organized societies began to form, decision-making expanded to cover more complex issues, including governance, trade, and resource management. In this environment, self-preservation meant ensuring not just the survival of the individual but also the health and prosperity of the community.

Emotional Influence on Decision-Making

Decision-making is greatly influenced by emotions, which frequently interact with instincts for self-preservation. In addition to being irrational forces, emotions are evolutionary processes that have aided in social cohesion and survival:

Fear and Caution: The strong feeling of fear is intimately related to the need for self-preservation. It encourages us to exercise caution in the face of potential risk, directing our decision-making away from dangerous or risky situations.

Empathy and Compassion: Positive emotions like empathy and compassion have developed over time to promote cooperation and improve social ties. These feelings frequently influence choices that put other people's needs ahead of one's own, indirectly aiding in social self-preservation.

Happiness and well-being: Positive emotions, like happiness and satisfaction, can improve judgment by encouraging innovation, problem-solving, and resilience. Being happy is in and of itself a sort of self-preservation.

Modern Decision-Making Obstacles to Self-Preservation

Although our emotions and instincts have developed to aid us in a variety of situations, the modern world has its own special complexity and dangers:

Information Overload: In the era of information, people are constantly being presented with options and data. This may overtax cognitive abilities, resulting in drowsy decision-making and poor choices.

Instant satisfaction has never been easier to obtain because of modern technologies. This may result in rash choices that put immediate pleasure ahead of long-term self-preservation.

Peer and social pressure: Social media and the digital age have made it easier for people to make decisions by amplifying social pressure. Instead of acting on their own self-preservation instincts, people may make decisions depending on social acceptance.

Risks related to the economy and technology: New risks are brought about by modern society's use of technology and financial investments. Making choices in these areas necessitates striking a balance between risk-taking and self-preservation.

Ethical dilemmas: In today's interconnected world, moral choices frequently require nuanced considerations of one's own survival, the welfare of society, and the environment. These issues can be difficult to balance.

Self-Preservation and Decision-Making Maze Navigation

Self-preservation and decision-making have a complex relationship that is shaped by millions of years of evolutionary history, impacted by our cognitive abilities, and affected by our emotional responses. We may balance our immediate survival instincts with logical, long-term decision-making by being aware of this link and making more informed decisions.

Self-preservation continues to be at the centre of our decision-making processes in the complicated world of today, where choices can range from routine everyday decisions to difficult ethical problems. We can make decisions with greater wisdom and purpose by developing our cognitive skills, strengthening our self-awareness, and taking into account the bigger picture. Ultimately, the extraordinary interaction between our reasoning minds and our primordial impulses is what allows us to make choices that advance our own well-being while respecting the well-being of others.

Making decisions that prioritize one's well-being and long-term goals while exercising self-preservation is an essential part of personal development. This subject examines many methods and tactics that can guide people through the decision-making process successfully.

The practice of critical thinking is a crucial part of self-preservation in decision-making. Making rational and reasoned decisions requires critical thinking skills such as information analysis, argument evaluation, and judgment. Individuals can make better decisions by developing these skills by evaluating the accuracy and dependability of the information they come across.

Another crucial element of self-preservation in decision-making is risk assessment. It entails weighing the advantages and disadvantages of several options. In order to make judgments that minimize potential harm and maximize potential rewards, this process forces people to think about the possibility and potential repercussions of each alternative.

Decision-making for self-preservation also requires careful consideration of prospective outcomes. This entails analyzing both the immediate and long-term effects of every decision. Individuals can make decisions that are in line with their beliefs, ambitions, and overall well-being by carefully weighing the possible outcomes.

There are specific ways that help improve self-preservation in decision-making in addition to these broad strategies. To better understand one's own values, aspirations, and objectives, people can, for instance, engage in mindfulness and self-reflection practices.

The practice of mindfulness entails being in the moment without passing judgment. It enables people to be aware of their ideas, feelings, and bodily sensations without getting sucked into them. By engaging in mindfulness practices, people can gain a deeper comprehension of their own thinking processes and emotional reactions, which can be extremely helpful when making decisions.

Contrarily, self-reflection entails taking the time to pause and consider one's own feelings, thoughts, and actions. It enables people to gain an understanding of their own drives, principles, and priorities. People can discover what is most important to them and what they want to give priority to when making decisions by engaging in self-reflection.

Individuals can develop clarity and insight into their own values, interests, and priorities by engaging in self-reflection and mindfulness practices. When making decisions, this self-awareness can act as a guide, assisting people in choosing decisions that are consistent with who they truly are.

Additionally, getting suggestions and opinions from dependable people can offer insightful and insightful viewpoints that help guide decision-making. People might learn new perspectives and take into account details they might have neglected by consulting mentors, friends, or experts in relevant subjects.

People who ask for guidance from reliable sources make themselves more receptive to fresh viewpoints and ideas. This can deepen their comprehension of a problem and aid in their decision-making. Trusted people can give advice, share their own experiences, and offer insightful commentary that can aid people in navigating difficult decision-making processes.

Individuals can profit from actively listening to various viewpoints in addition to asking for advice. People can better comprehend the numerous aspects influencing a decision by having frank and open discussions. Before making a decision, they might use this to analyze the benefits and cons of several points of view.

In order to protect oneself when making decisions, one must be aware of and in control of cognitive biases. These biases are inborn mental heuristics that can result in erroneous choices. Confirmation bias, availability bias, and anchoring bias are examples of prevalent biases that people can reduce the influence of and use to make more objective decisions.

For instance, confirmation bias is the propensity to look for data that supports one's previous thoughts or opinions. People may reject or disregard evidence that conflicts with their preconceived views, which can result in a narrow-minded approach to decision-making. People can actively seek out different ideas and take into consideration alternate viewpoints by being aware of their confirmation bias.

On the other hand, availability bias is the propensity to base decisions on information that is easily accessible. This may cause you to miss out on crucial but difficult-to-find information. Individuals might attempt to obtain thorough and impartial information before making a decision by becoming aware of availability bias.

Another prevalent cognitive bias that may influence decision-making is anchoring bias. It entails making decisions based primarily on the initial piece of information we come upon. This may result in the original information having an undue influence and skewinging the decision-making process. People can intentionally analyze a variety of facts and prevent being unduly swayed by first impressions by being aware of anchoring bias.

In conclusion, self-preservation in decision-making is a complex subject that includes a range of tactics and strategies. People can make informed and logical decisions that put their well-being and long-term objectives first by cultivating critical thinking abilities, performing risk assessments, considering probable outcomes, practising self-reflection, getting help, and minimizing cognitive biases.

SELF-PRESERVATION IN PERSONAL SAFETY AND WELL-BEING

A fundamental part of human nature is the need to protect one's own safety and well-being. It includes a broad range of actions, choices, and tactics meant to protect one's physical, mental, and emotional well-being. Beyond basic survival, the idea of self-preservation includes the desire for a happy and secure life. In this thorough investigation, we delve into the many facets of self-preservation in personal safety and well-being, analyzing its significance, the difficulties it encounters, and methods for successful self-preservation in the complicated world of today.

The urge to protect oneself

Self-preservation is a fundamental drive that is entrenched throughout the biology of every living thing. It serves as the impetus for actions that protect safety and survival. This instinct can appear in several ways:

Fight or Flight Response: The body's fight-or-flight response is triggered when a threat is recognized. An individual can use this physiological response to either face the threat or run away from it. Greater heart rate, greater awareness, and the release of stress hormones like adrenaline are all aspects of it.

Simple reflexes, like removing one's hand from a burning surface or blinking in response to an object suddenly moving toward the eye, are automatic defences intended to stop harm.

Pain Sensation: The experience of pain alerts a person to a potential injury and acts as a warning sign. An immediate reaction to pain is to get out of harm's way.

Basic Needs: Self-preservation can be seen in the quest for necessities like food, water, and shelter. Physical survival depends on having access to these essentials.

Emotional Well-Being: Emotional reactions like fear, worry, and grief can spur actions that safeguard emotional well-being. Self-preservation involves avoiding events that make people feel upset.

Physical self-preservation and personal safety

Physical self-preservation entails taking steps and making decisions that will protect one's physical well-being. It includes a variety of tactics:

Safety precautions: It is essential for physical self-preservation to take safety precautions to avoid mishaps and injury. This includes taking precautions like using seatbelts, wearing helmets, and driving safely.

Self-defence: Acquiring self-defence skills can enable someone to defend themselves against physical assaults or threats.

Healthcare: Proactive steps to maintain physical health and avoid sickness include routine medical checkups, screenings, and vaccines.

Diet and exercise: Choosing a healthy diet and getting regular exercise are crucial for physical self-preservation. They increase general health and lower the likelihood of developing chronic illnesses.

Avoiding substance abuse is essential for maintaining physical health. This includes abstaining from the abuse of drugs and alcohol. Abuse of substances can result in addiction, health issues, and accidents.

Protecting one's mental and emotional health

Strategies to preserve one's mental and emotional well-being are part of mental and emotional self-preservation. The following factor is equally essential for general well-being:

Effective stress reduction methods, such as meditation, deep breathing exercises, and relaxation techniques, assist in lessening the detrimental effects of stress on mental and emotional health.

Emotional Awareness: Acquiring emotional intelligence and awareness enables people to properly identify and control their emotions. This ability is essential for preserving emotional equilibrium.

Social Support: Keeping up good relationships with others and asking friends and family for help might help you be emotionally stable and resilient when things are tough.

Counselling and Therapy: Seeking professional assistance through counselling or therapy while dealing with mental health issues is a useful way to protect oneself. It offers methods and tactics for overcoming emotional challenges.

Set and uphold healthy boundaries in partnerships to safeguard each other's emotional well-being. Burnout and emotional exploitation are avoided.

Challenges to Personal Safety in the Modern World

Self-preservation in terms of personal safety and well-being faces particular difficulties in the modern world:

Distractions from technology and the internet: These factors put people's personal safety at risk. For instance, distracted driving puts everyone's safety at risk.

Mental health stigma still exists despite increased awareness, which can prevent people from getting assistance when they need it.

Environmental Risks: Environmental issues like climate change and natural disasters raise fresh safety issues that call for preventative actions.

Cybersecurity: In a world that is becoming more and more digital, personal safety also includes cybersecurity. Self-preservation is essential in protecting one's digital identity and personal data.

Effective Self-Preservation Techniques

A proactive attitude is necessary for effective self-preservation in terms of personal safety and well-being. Here are some tactics to think about:

Assess potential dangers and hazards in your environment on a regular basis. This involves assessing cybersecurity dangers, emotional pressures, and physical safety hazards.

Learn the knowledge and abilities required for self-preservation through education and training. This may entail studying topics like first aid, mental health, cybersecurity, and personal safety.

Prioritize a healthy lifestyle that includes a balanced diet, consistent exercise, enough sleep, and stress reduction techniques.

Develop routines for mindfulness and self-care to improve your emotional well-being. Hobbies, journaling, and meditation are some activities that can help you feel emotionally balanced.

Social Support System: Uphold wholesome relationships with friends and family. In times of hardship, social assistance is an essential resource.

Don't be afraid to seek expert assistance if you are having problems with your bodily or mental health. Early action can stop problems from getting worse.

Prepare for emergencies by assembling emergency supplies, making evacuation plans, and remaining knowledgeable about potential dangers in your area.

Cybersecurity Awareness: Inform yourself about potential hazards online and take precautions when using the internet. Consider using cybersecurity software and creating strong, one-of-a-kind passwords.

Emotional intelligence's function

Emotional intelligence (EI) is essential for maintaining one's own safety and well-being. Emotional intelligence (EI) is the capacity to perceive, comprehend, control, and use emotions in oneself and in interpersonal interactions. It is an essential ability for making choices that protect one's safety and well-being. The following are some ways that emotional intelligence aids in self-preservation:

Self-awareness: Self-awareness is the starting point for emotional intelligence. Making decisions that prioritize one's well-being requires awareness of and comprehension of one's own emotions, stressors, and triggers. For instance, recognizing burnout in a high-stress job may motivate someone to look for a better work-life balance.

Emotional Intelligence (EI) includes the capacity for successful emotion regulation. When presented with difficult situations, this ability can be very helpful in controlling stress and making defensible decisions. When faced with a crisis, the ability to maintain composure under pressure is essential for personal safety.

Empathy: Empathy, a facet of EI, enables people to comprehend the feelings and viewpoints of others. This talent is vital for creating and maintaining healthy relationships, which contribute greatly to emotional well-being and safety.

EI contributes to conflict resolution in its own right. Conflicts can be handled more skillfully by people with high emotional intelligence, which lowers the risk of negative effects on their physical or mental health.

Making decisions: People with emotional intelligence are better able to make choices that are consistent with their beliefs and well-being. They have the capacity to balance emotional reactions with logical considerations, leading to decisions that put long-term security and happiness first.

In the Digital Age, Self-Preservation

The emergence of the digital era has brought with it a slew of fresh difficulties and chances for self-preservation in terms of personal safety and well-being. The online world has become a fundamental aspect of daily life, bringing both threats and benefits:

Cybersecurity: Safeguarding digital assets and personal data is a contemporary method of self-preservation. It is crucial to take precautions to avoid identity theft, cyberbullying, and online fraud.

The use of social media may have an effect on one's mental and emotional health. It's essential to be aware of one's digital footprint and to avoid hazardous content.

Digital gadget use, in particular, might have a negative impact on physical health when it comes to excessive screen time. Controlling screen time is crucial for maintaining physical health.

Online relationships: Keeping up with them may be both rewarding and difficult. Setting limits online and creating a support system are crucial components of self-preservation.

Digital detox: Interrupting one's use of technology on a regular basis can help one's mental and emotional health. The incessant demands of the internet world can be interrupted by doing this.

Self-Preservation Obstacles in Personal Safety and Well-Being

Despite the significance of self-preservation, people encounter a number of barriers and difficulties in their quest for safety and well-being:

Procrastination: Procrastination can make it more difficult to protect oneself. Neglecting self-care practices or delaying key decisions might jeopardize safety and well-being.

Peer Pressure: Social pressures and peer influence may cause people to make decisions that are not in their best interests. Peer pressure can cause dangerous behaviours or undermine moral principles.

Lack of Resources: A lack of resources, such as those for money, education, or healthcare, can make it difficult to protect oneself. Economic inequalities can make it harder for someone to put their own well-being first.

Mental Health Stigma: The stigma associated with mental health problems might prevent people from getting care when they need it. Untreated mental health issues can result from this, which can have an impact on general well-being.

Overcommitting: People may not have enough time or energy to devote to self-preservation if they over-commit to their work, families, or social responsibilities. Burnout and a decline in well-being may come from this.

Self-Preservation Techniques for Personal Safety and Well-Being

It takes conscious tactics and intentional efforts to overcome these obstacles and promote self-preservation in terms of personal safety and well-being. The following are effective methods that encourage self-preservation:

Make self-care a priority by setting aside time for activities that support your physical, emotional, and psychological well-being. Exercise, relaxation methods, pastimes, and introspection are a few examples of this.

Set Boundaries: To safeguard your time, energy, and well-being, set boundaries in both your personal and professional lives. To avoid taking on too much, learn to say no when it's appropriate.

Stress management: To deal with life's obstacles and lessen the negative effects of stress on well-being, develop effective stress management strategies like yoga, meditation, or mindfulness.

When faced with difficulties or mental anguish, don't be afraid to ask friends, family, or professionals for support. The act of asking for assistance is not a sign of weakness.

Fostering good connections that offer emotional support and improve general well-being is an investment. With poisonous or damaging relationships, establish boundaries.

Financial literacy: To ensure your financial security and future financial goals, develop sound financial planning skills.

Time management: Manage your time well to balance your personal, professional, and self-care obligations. Schedule time for activities that enhance well-being and safety.

Prioritize your mental health by getting the help you need, such as counselling or therapy. Eliminate the stigma surrounding mental health and give your emotional well-being a top priority.

Digital Well-being: Manage your screen time, safeguard your personal information, and develop a positive relationship with technology to practice digital well-being.

Risk assessment: Constantly evaluate risks and make wise choices that put your safety and well-being first. Ask a specialist for guidance when making important decisions in your life.

The Self-Preservation Obligation

It takes a combination of intuition, self-awareness, emotional intelligence, and conscious choices to maintain one's own safety and well-being. It is a crucial component of human existence, ensuring that people live full lives in a tough and complex world.

People can prioritize their safety and well-being by recognizing the complex nature of self-preservation, comprehending the difficulties it poses, and using appropriate techniques. Self-preservation ultimately demonstrates the intrinsic importance we place on our own lives and happiness by motivating us to make decisions that safeguard, protect, and further our bodily, emotional, and psychological well-being.

Self-defense in times of need

Emergency self-defence is a critical component of one's personal safety and well-being. This subject explores methods for keeping secure and coming to swift decisions in a variety of emergency scenarios, such as accidents or natural catastrophes. It looks at how being prepared for emergencies, knowing how to administer first aid, and having survival skills may help one stay alive and keep others safe. It looks at how anxiety, fear, and panic can affect judgment, and it offers techniques for remaining cool and collected under pressure. People frequently experience elevated levels of stress and panic when faced with emergencies, which can impair their cognition and limit their capacity to make logical judgments. People can better negotiate these difficult situations and make choices that boost their chances of survival by understanding the psychological dynamics at work.

Being ready can make a huge difference in an emergency. This subject highlights the value of having an effective emergency plan in place. It discusses crucial actions to do prior to, during, and following an emergency, such as assembling an emergency kit, being aware of evacuation routes, and setting up communication channels with family members.

This subject looks at the value of first aid training under dire circumstances. It offers comprehensive details on fundamental first aid procedures, including CPR, wound treatment, and treating typical injuries. By having these abilities, people can efficiently respond to medical situations and give others in need prompt assistance.

Another essential component of self-preservation in emergencies is survival knowledge. This subject explores a number of survival skills, including locating shelter, sanitizing water, and hunting for food. It highlights how crucial it is to comprehend one's surroundings and make use of the resources at hand in order to survive until aid arrives.

The psychological component of self-preservation in emergencies is covered in this issue. It examines how anxiety, fear, and panic affect our ability to make decisions and offers techniques for remaining composed and sensible under pressure. People can improve their decision-making and boost their chances of survival by being aware of the psychological dynamics at work.

Stress causes the body to release hormones like adrenaline, which can start the fight-or-flight response in some people. This reaction is a biological survival strategy that gets the body ready to face or run from danger. However, this reaction can occasionally result in impulsive and unreasonable choices in emergency situations. Understanding how stress affects the body and mind allows people to control their stress levels and make better-informed decisions.

Another strong feeling that might affect decision-making in an emergency is fear. Fear can cause a variety of reactions, such as freezing, running away, or fighting when a life is in danger. These innate reactions can take precedence over logical thought. However, people may learn to manage their fear and make choices that put their safety and well-being first by learning how fear influences decision-making.

Another element that might have a big impact on emergency decision-making is panic. Extreme fear and anxiety, which are the hallmarks of panic, are frequently accompanied by a lack of control and sane reasoning. Panic can swiftly spread among people in emergency situations, causing a mess and confusion. People can take action to stay calm and composed and be able to make better decisions if they are aware of the nature of panic and its potential effects.

People can use a variety of tactics to stay composed and sensible under pressure. Deep breathing and relaxation exercises are one such tactic. People can lower their stress levels and recover control over their emotions by taking slow, deep breaths and concentrating on soothing thoughts. Additionally, mindfulness training and present-moment awareness can support people in maintaining attention and rational decision-making.

In an emergency, self-preservation goes beyond what one person does. The significance of community readiness and cooperation during disasters is emphasized by this issue. Communities that are well-prepared for catastrophes and have robust social networks are more likely to respond and recover in an efficient manner. Individuals can improve their chances of surviving and recovering by encouraging a sense of collective resilience. Initiatives like neighbourhood watch programs, community emergency response teams, and disaster preparedness training can help achieve this.

In times of crisis, it's important to pool resources and provide a hand to one another. Resources like food, water, and shelter may become limited during emergencies. Individuals may guarantee that everyone's fundamental requirements are covered by cooperating and pooling their resources. Community organizations, networks of mutual aid, and coordination with local authorities can all help with this.

Emergency self-preservation includes the psychological component of making choices while under pressure, fear, or panic. People can improve their decision-making and raise their chances of survival by comprehending these psychological aspects and using tactics to manage them. Cooperation and community readiness are also essential for self-preservation in calamities. People can increase their chances of surviving and recovering by encouraging a sense of communal resilience and helping one another. Self-preservation in times of crisis is not selfish; rather, it is essential since it gives people the knowledge and abilities to safeguard both themselves and others, ensuring their safety and survival.

CONCLUSION

In the grand tapestry of life, the threads of self-preservation weave a pattern of survival, resilience, and growth. As we journey through the pages of this book, we have explored the many facets of self-preservation, from the primal instincts that drive us to survive to the complex strategies we employ to thrive in various aspects of our lives.

We have delved into the evolutionary basis of self-preservation, understanding how this instinct has shaped our behaviours and decision-making processes. We have examined the physical techniques of self-defence, acknowledging the importance of protecting our physical selves in a world that can sometimes pose threats.

We have navigated the labyrinth of mental and emotional self-preservation, learning how to maintain our well-being amidst the storms of stress and emotional upheaval. We have learned to set healthy boundaries in our relationships, to protect ourselves from toxicity and abuse, and to foster connections that nourish our souls.

We have ventured into different environments, understanding how to preserve ourselves in the workplace, online spaces, and during emergencies. We have explored the realm of financial self-preservation, learning the importance of financial stability and security in our overall well-being.

We have journeyed through the landscape of health and wellness, understanding the importance of maintaining our physical health through exercise, nutrition, and preventive healthcare measures. We have also learned the importance of mental and emotional well-being and the strategies we can employ to promote it.

We have delved into the realm of personal development, understanding how self-preservation plays a crucial role in our personal growth and self-improvement. We have explored decision-making, learning how to make informed and rational decisions that serve our best interests.

We have navigated the complex world of social interactions, learning effective communication skills, conflict resolution techniques, and strategies for building and maintaining healthy relationships. We have ventured into the digital age, understanding the importance of cybersecurity and online privacy in our increasingly digital world.

We have explored the realm of emergencies, learning how to stay safe and make quick decisions when faced with natural disasters or accidents. We have delved into the workplace, learning how to maintain a healthy work-life balance and deal with workplace stress.

We have explored personal relationships, learning how to maintain healthy boundaries and self-care within our friendships and romantic partnerships. We have journeyed into the realm of parenting, understanding how to balance our needs with those of our children and how to practice self-care as a parent.

In this journey, we have learned that self-preservation is not a selfish act but a necessity. It is the foundation upon which we build our lives, the armour that protects us as we navigate the world and the compass that guides us toward growth and fulfilment.

As we close this book, let us carry these lessons with us. Let us remember that self-preservation is a heroic act, a testament to our resilience and strength. It is the flame that burns within us, lighting our path as we journey through life.

May this book serve as a beacon, illuminating the path of self-preservation. May it empower you to protect yourself, to nurture your well-being, and to thrive in all aspects of your life. In the end, self-preservation is not just about surviving but about flourishing in our own unique, beautiful ways.

And so, as we turn the final page, let us step forward with courage, armed with the knowledge and strategies we have gained. Self-preservation is not just a necessity but a heroic journey of survival, resilience, and growth. And in this journey, we are not alone. For as long as we preserve ourselves, we preserve the essence of being human."